KiDS CREATE!

For a free color catalog describing Gareth Stevens Publishing's list of high-quality books and multimedia programs, call 1-800-542-2595 (USA) or 1-800-461-9120 (Canada).
Gareth Stevens Publishing's Fax: (414) 225-0377.
See our catalog, too, on the World Wide Web: gsinc.com

Library of Congress Cataloging-in-Publication Data

Carlson, Laurie M., 1952-
    Kids create! / by Laurie Carlson.
        p. cm. (Williamson kids can!)
    Includes bibliographical references and index.
    Summary: A collection of art and craft projects for creative self-expression using readily available materials and accompanied by easy-to-follow instructions.
    ISBN 0-8368-2232-3 (lib. bdg.)
    1. Handicraft—Juvenile literature. [1. Handicraft.]
I. Title. II. Series.
TT160.C354   1998
745.5—dc21   98-13031

First published in this edition in North America in 1999 by
Gareth Stevens Publishing
1555 North RiverCenter Drive, Suite 201
Milwaukee, WI 53212 USA

Original © 1990 by Laurie Carlson. This library edition published by arrangement with Williamson Publishing Company, P.O. Box 185, Charlotte, VT 05445. Illustrations by Loretta Trezzo-Braren. Project diagrams by Laurie Carlson. Additional end matter © 1999 by Gareth Stevens, Inc. Original paperback edition of this book is available through Williamson Publishing, 1-800-234-8791.

Williamson Kids Can!® is a registered trademark of Williamson Publishing Company.

Printed in the United States of America

1 2 3 4 5 6 7 8 9 03 02 01 00 99

• Metric Table •

1 inch = 2.54 centimeters
1 pound = .4536 kilogram
1 cup = 240 milliliters/225 grams
°C = (°F – 32°) ÷ 1.8
1 teaspoon = 5 milliliters
1 tablespoon = 15 milliliters
1 foot = .3048 meter
1 gallon = 3.784 liters
$1.00 (U.S.) = $1.58 (Canadian) in Fall, 1998

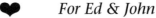

For Ed & John

KiDS CREATE!

Art & Craft Experiences for 3- to 9-Year-Olds

Laurie Carlson

Gareth Stevens Publishing
MILWAUKEE

A Williamson Kids Can!® Book. This library edition published by arrangement with Williamson Publishing Company.

KIDS CREATE!

CONTENTS

KiDS CREATE!

KIDS CREATE! is a collection of art and craft projects for children ages 4 through 9 years. The younger children will need quite a bit of guidance in using the materials, but they will benefit from the fun of using different mediums, as well as the practice in refining their motor skills. Children in the mid-range may be able to read the instructions themselves and will very likely be able to follow the illustrations. These children, too, will benefit from the help and input of an adult. Older children may well be able to use this book on their own, perhaps asking for some guidance in assembling materials and in using hot glue, craft knives, and paraffin.

Most of the materials are readily available in many homes. Feel free to substitute wherever needed as these items are merely suggestions. As much as possible, I have tried to avoid using materials which are harmful to the environment. No project uses specially purchased styrofoam items. In some cases, I mention items such as trays used to package meats. Obviously, we need to work toward ridding our environment

of these harmful packaging materials, but since they are presently still widely available, rather than throw them away, save them to recycle in various art and craft projects. In fact, it is a good idea to collect these trays as well as egg cartons to give to school craft programs. At the very least, this will keep these items out of our landfills. Plastic wrap has been omitted from every project. There are many suitable substitutes. *Art and craft projects should be environmentally friendly*; part of the creativity for children should involve finding and using biodegradable materials whose production and disposal are environmentally sound.

Why Kids Love Arts and Crafts

The joy of creating something is exhilarating. Children, especially, enjoy the creative process, loving every minute of the making. Creative thinking and personal emotion combine into an individual's artistic expression–a kind of expression where there is no right or wrong.

Making art fulfills children's real need for self-expression. They are eager to experience life and to participate actively and imaginatively in it.

Children crave the creative outlet that making things provides. We cheat them if we only offer them a life of television and other passive activities. Children who are deprived of opportunities for self-expression through the arts often seek other emotional and creative outlets. Behavior, dress, and interests reflect this unmet need. Street graffiti, unusual hairstyles and strong identification with peer groups become the only available form of self-expression.

The zest for art is easy to recognize in young children. It doesn't disappear as they get older, as some would have you think. It isn't a phase that children outgrow. The desire to express oneself is on-going, still present at all ages. Unfortunately as we get older, we become more inhibited. We begin to judge our efforts as compared to some idea of perfection that we hold. We forget that we can create just for the fun of it.

Children ages 3-9 still feel very free to express themselves artistically. Any form of hesitation or withdrawal usually has more to do with factors other than the task at hand. If we, as adults, continually provide these younger children with opportunities to refine their motor skills, to become familiar with various media, to feel proud of each and every creation, we give to our children multiple gifts. They are more likely to approach the preteen and teen years with greater confidence and a valuable awareness that artistic expression is a pleasurable, available, acceptable creative and emotional outlet.

As you discover, along with your children, the freedom and adventure that art can provide, leave inhibitions behind and have fun! The value of the activity isn't measured in the finished product, but rather in the pure enjoyment and learning along the way.

Using This Book

Some of us adults have allowed our creative impulses to become stifled. We feel we lack the imagination and freedom to lead our children in creating art. For us, I've included some structured projects in this book. Use them as a springboard for your own ideas and variations. Use the suggested project design as a starting point, not as a rigid parameter to be strictly copied. When a pattern is shown, it's to give you a suggested size or shape. If you want to try a project in the book but lack something on the materials list, don't hesitate to look for something that could be substituted. Except for the clay dough recipes, there really are no absolutes; using different materials can result in a wider variety of experiences.

Use the ideas in this book as a starting point for your own creative expression, as well as the children's. Experiment, change, and push the limits of each project or media you try. As adults we tend to let our lack of creative confidence limit what we try. Urge yourself to try new materials and different ways of using them. By conveying an attitude of capable confidence toward making art, your children will sense that they, too, are free to explore and create. Refrain from criticizing your own efforts or your child's. If something turns out differently than you had planned, greet it as a great innovation, not a grave disappointment. Avoid even thinking in terms of failure, or a right or wrong way, or even

 DANGER ZONES

To ensure the safety and well-being of your young artists and artisans, please observe these safety measures.

Paraffin: Wax and paraffin should be melted in a can placed in the top of a double boiler (water in both parts of double boiler). An adult must always do this part of a project. Paraffin is flammable.

Hot glue gun: These are very handy, but must be used by adults only.

Balloons: Balloons may seem innocent and fun, but they can be deadly to toddlers who swallow deflated balloons or balloon pieces. Please use with care around young children.

Craft knives: Adults should use the craft knives and sharp scissors, demonstrating correct methods for safe use and handling.

Ventilation: Proper ventilation is necessary when using rubber cement and many fixatives. Acrylic sprays are extremely flammable as well as toxic. (Hair spray is a good substitute.) Adults should spray fixatives, not children.

a better way. Children pick up these unspoken messages, leading them to criticize their work as well as to doubt their ability.

Remember, there are no rights or wrongs—no failures—in crafting. Every time a child tries something, he or she is enlarging a skills repertoire and increasing the scope of creative thinking. For all of us the possibilities are always endless. So enjoy, encourage, and excite yourself and your child with art. The world gives us all so many restrictions, criticisms and putdowns. Let creating together be a door you help your child open; a door to personal satisfaction, pride and enjoyment. Along the way you and your child can enjoy some truly quality time together: exploring ideas, creating from within, laughing together, and patting one another on the back.

Let the joy and excitement of creating something of their own give your children the confidence and courage to hold on to the creative innocence of childhood for a lifetime.

Use the ideas in this book to unlock your own creative processes. As you become more confident about providing creative opportunities for your child, you will be able to adapt and expand these beginnings into a multitude of ideas involving a variety of media.

Now, find those scissors, mix the paint, turn on your imagination, and let's begin!

★ KEYS TO CONFIDENCE ★

Each project is identified as to the approximate degree of difficulty involved in confidently completing it. Look for the paint brushes to identify the suggested range of ability or dexterity each project might involve.

1 brush= Few fine motor skills needed. Adults may need to help very young children by preparing some of the materials ahead of time. With very little adult assistance these projects should delight most children.

2 brushes= Skills such as cutting, folding, using a template or painting may be required. Young children need practice with these skills, but adults should avoid creating frustrating experiences for those truly too young to handle them. Most children enjoy these projects, and will experiment with the wider range of mediums and tools.

3 brushes= More involved projects that require manual dexterity and a variety of steps to completion.

Clock Watchers

Because time allowances are necessary for using some mediums and completing some of the projects, I've identified those projects requiring more than one hour to complete. Look for the little clock which is your signal that this project takes more than one hour. Read through these projects because many of them have convenient stopping points. If you can leave your materials out and come back later, the time may not be a factor.

In some cases, materials must be prepared ahead of time, or a drying or baking time is required. This is not included in the hour estimate. Allow extra time for drying which varies with the medium used, as well as thickness of the projects, humidity levels and temperatures.

★

These keys are quite arbitrary. Don't let them limit your choice of project. If a project is interesting, fun and appropriate in nature, work around any part that seems beyond the children. Kids are extremely versatile, especially when they really want to do something. Usually they are very willing to stretch their abilities or find clever shortcuts.

PAPER & PASTE

The first craft material most children are introduced to is paper. It's easy for even the youngest child to manipulate paper by folding, cutting and scribbling. When paste is added, the possibilities are endless. The types and varieties of papers available provide many different ways to do a project. Keep a box for storing the unusual papers you find: gift wrap, tissue, cellophane, lightweight cardboard, textured grass cloth, embossed wallpapers, crepe paper, waxed paper, even computer printout papers (useful for painting banners or drawing murals). Keep this assortment of papers handy, letting children experiment with folding, cutting and pasting the different types.

Pastes and Glues

Pastes and glues vary in their kinds and uses, too. The *school pastes* are not used as much as in the past, because they are thick, hard to spread, and crumble when dry. They are, however, inexpensive and don't spill. *White glue* is a favorite with children. It is washable and can be diluted with water to make spreading easier for young fingers. It dries clear. *Glue sticks* are handy for small projects that need a small amount of adhesive. *Rubber cement* is useful for mounting papers on mat board for display. It dries smooth, leaving no bumps beneath the paper. It doesn't apply easily though, because it dries so quickly. An uncovered container will dry out very quickly. Rubber cement is more practical for an older child's use. *Hot glue guns* are useful for many craft projects. They definitely require an adult's supervision because they can be dangerous. The gun and glue reach high temperatures that can easily burn young hands.

Scissors and Other Tools

There are some other tools that make creating with paper easier and widen the possibilities. You'll want to have several types of scissors: *safety scissors* for the young child, *pointed scissors* for the older ones who need to snip in tiny areas. *Pinking shears* are fun to use, too. For cutting heavy cardboard and other craft materials a *craft knife* is desirable. Craft knives come in a variety of designs. They are all sharp and should only be used by the adult who is assisting the child. Even older children need adult direction and supervision when using them. Other tools you'll find useful are *hole punches, staplers, rulers, metal brads and paper clips.*

Pre-school children need lots of practice honing their fine motor skills. Safety scissors and scraps of paper will keep them busy. Encourage these children to cut in different ways, creating shapes and patterns with the paper. Show them how to draw a line, and then cut along it.

This gives them practice at eye-hand coordination, an important skill needed for later school success.

Simply cutting papers into geometric shapes can be fun and challenging for the older child as well. Find examples of fine paper-cutting, called scherenschnitte, in a library book, and encourage them to try the delicate craft using nail scissors and rice paper.

Paper can also be cut into strips, rolled into coils, then glued down to create designs. Called quilling, it is a project that can vary in difficulty depending upon the age and ability of the artist.

Just playing with papers, pastes and a few tools should get creative juices flowing. Read on for a few ideas you might not have thought of, then get out the box of supplies and see what you can come up with. Remember, most papers are inexpensive, so feel free to experiment and let your child try things you and I might not have considered.

# SEND A LETTER

Quill Pen

✂ MATERIALS ✂

Bird feather (chicken or turkey feathers are best)

Sharp knife or scissors

Ink or thinned tempera paint

What's the first thing you'll need in order to send a special letter? Of course, it's a pen! Here's how to make a real quill pen to sign your John Hancock — otherwise known as your name.

With a knife or scissors, cut a slant at the tip of the feather's quill. This slant allows the ink to flow down from the quill to the paper, when you press the feather to paper.

To load the pen, dip the cut part of the feather into ink or tempera paint thinned with a little water. Practice writing on scrap paper first. Keep a paper towel handy to blot excess ink.

If your quill pen tip gets worn down, cut a bit more off, at a slant, and it will be new again.

Cut the feather at a slant.

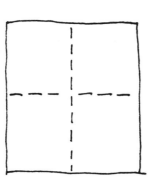

Fold the letter twice.

Place letter or card in the center of envelope paper.

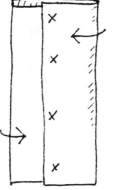

Fold side in and glue.

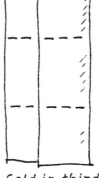

Fold in thirds.

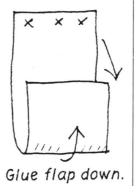

Glue flap down.

Envelopes Are Easy

✂ MATERIALS ✂

Paper

Scissors

White glue, glue stick or paste

Envelopes can be made from almost any type of paper: gift wrap, shopping bags, aluminum foil, colored papers, wallpaper sample pages, or typing paper.

Before making an envelope, write the letter or create the card you want to put in it. Then make it to fit the size you need.

To create an envelope, use a piece of paper the size of your letter. Fold the letter once each way and lay it across the envelope paper. Fold the two sides around the letter and glue. Fold in thirds from top to bottom. Fold up from the bottom. Use some glue to dot the edges of the top flap and fold it over. Press.

To create an envelope for a card, use paper four times the size of the card, and lay the card the same as you did the letter.

CREATE A POP-UP CARD

Paper

Glue

Scissors

Crayons, markers or paints

One type of pop-up card is made from a piece of 8" x 10" paper. Fold it in half length-wise. Cut out a 3" x 3" notch. Fold the remaining portion that juts out down inside the card at an angle. This will be the piece that pops up when the card is opened. Cut into any shape such as a heart, or cut into an oval with a face drawn on it. Decorate the front cover of the card as you wish, and add your message.

Another pop-up card is made with construction paper and paste or glue. Make a greeting card. Decide what design you want to pop up from your card. Some ideas are: balloon shapes, a birthday cake, a sun, a heart, Christmas designs, or a message bubble. Draw and color the pop-up piece on a separate piece of paper. Cut it out. Cut a small strip of paper, about 1/2" wide and 3" long. Fold accordion-style, in small folds. Glue one end to position inside the card. Trim the strip so it pops up about 1". Glue your cut-out design to the other end of the strip.

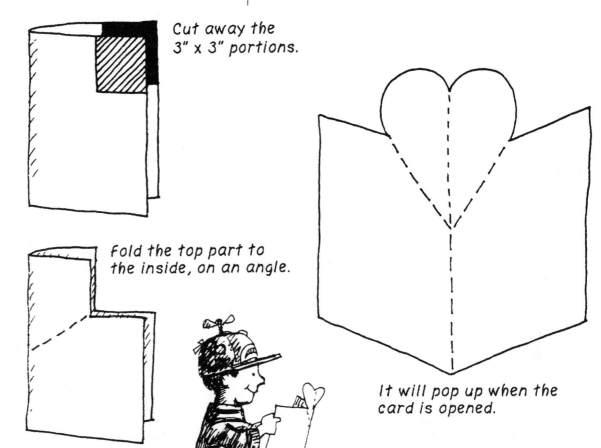

Cut away the 3" x 3" portions.

Fold the top part to the inside, on an angle.

It will pop up when the card is opened.

It's easy to make a bound book for writing poetry, stories, or to use as a journal to record your thoughts on life.

✂ MATERIALS ✂

Cardboard: two pieces of $6\frac{1}{4}$" x $9\frac{1}{4}$", one piece of $\frac{1}{2}$" x $9\frac{1}{4}$"

Fabric: 11" x 15 $\frac{1}{2}$"

Typing paper: 25 sheets

Scissors

Needle

Thread

Ruler

Special gift wrap paper for the inside cover (optional)

White glue

Lay the piece of fabric on a table with the wrong side facing up. Position the cardboard pieces as shown. The small piece of cardboard will be the book's spine. Leave a $\frac{1}{8}$" space between the spine and the other pieces of cardboard to make it easy to turn the pages.

Spread glue on the back of the cardboard and reposition on the fabric. Press into place firmly. Let dry.

Turn the edges of fabric up over the cardboard. Fold the corners in to miter them (neatly at an angle). Glue down. Let dry.

Using 5 pieces of typing paper at a time, fold the papers in half. Stitch them together with the needle and thread down the creased middle. You will have 5 of these little booklets. Stack them together, with the stitched spines touching. Apply glue to the spines and cover with a heavy weight, such as a telephone book. Dry.

Place the book pages on the cover spine.

For the inside cover or flyleaf, decorate some typing paper or use something special such as gift wrap. This will be the decorative inside cover of your book. Cut two flyleaf papers to 8" x 11" each. Place the flyleaf sheets over the book, and cover and glue to the first page of the book. Repeat at the last page and back inside cover. This will hold the book together.

Now, start writing! ✒

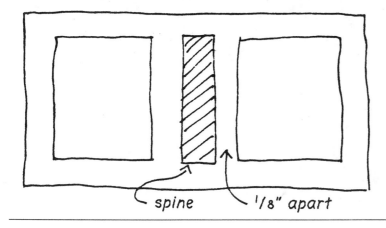

spine ← → $\frac{1}{8}$" apart

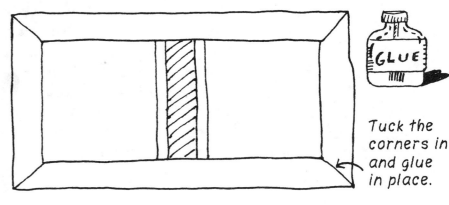

GLUE

Tuck the corners in and glue in place.

✂ MATERIALS ✂

Poster or magazine picture

Rubber cement

Lightweight cardboard
(notebook covers, tagboard,
shirt cardboard)

Scissors

Clear adhesive paper if desired
(like Contact® brand)

Glue picture to
the cardboard.

Trim the cardboard so it is the same size as the picture. Spread the back of the picture with rubber cement, and glue to the cardboard. Dry. Turn the cardboard over and use a pencil to draw curving lines from one edge of the cardboard to the other. Draw more curving shapes within the larger ones. Don't make the areas too small, or cutting them out will be difficult. When you have divided the area into interesting shapes, cut along the lines to create the puzzle pieces.

Store pieces in an envelope. If you want to make the puzzle more durable, cover the picture with a piece of clear adhesive paper before cutting.

If you make several puzzles, you may want to label them so they don't get mixed up. Label the pieces that go with each puzzle by marking all pieces to the same puzzle with a similar mark such as a colored "x" on the back of one puzzle's pieces, an "s" on all pieces to another puzzle.

Draw a puzzle pattern
on the cardboard.
Cut the puzzle apart
on the lines.

MATERIALS ✄ ✄

Lightweight cardboard or tagboard

Colored markers

Scissors

Draw and cut out several basic hanger shapes using the pattern shown. Use the marking pens to decorate, draw and write messages on the hangers. Some ideas you might want to use are:

DO NOT DISTURB
NO ADULTS ALLOWED
ON VACATION
maid service
GREAT BRAIN AT WORK
Home of the Main Brain
QUIET-KID AT WORK

Door Knob Hanger Pattern

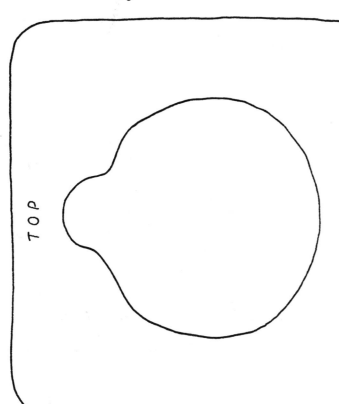

TOP

BOTTOM

✂ MATERIALS ✂

Blender

Warm water
(room temperature will work)

Rolling pin

2-3 towels

Steam iron

2 plastic dishpans (same size), bottoms cut out with a craft knife.

2 pieces of wire window screen, cut to fit the bottom of the dishpans

1 larger dishpan (or sink), for draining the excess water

Bedsheet piece, about 12" x 12"

Newspapers, torn in 1" x 2" strips*

One-half of a full-size double sheet of newspaper seems to be all a blender can handle at one time. It yields paper approximately 8" x 8". Don't use the advertising sections that are printed on slick colored paper, as the finish won't allow the paper to absorb water.

Fill the blender ²/₃ full of warm water. While blending at low speed, drop strips of newspaper in, one at a time through the lid. Blend until thick and pulpy. Place the screens over the opening of the dishpans. Set the dishpans inside each other and over the third, larger dishpan (or sink) to drain.

Slowly pour the pulp onto the screen. Allow water to drain off. Remove the screens. The pulp will stick to the top one. Place the pulp mass, screen side down, on a towel. Cover the pulp with the other screen. Roll gently but firmly with a rolling pin, to squeeze out more water. Now gently peel the pulp from the screen. Lay it on a flat towel. Cover with an old piece of sheet or a thin towel, and iron to remove more moisture. Let paper dry overnight.

If you want to add some color to your paper, use torn colored shopping bags instead of newspapers. You can also add objects, such as feathers, flower petals, confetti to give different textures and interesting effects. If you place a flat object under the pulp mass before it is ironed, you can emboss a design on the finished paper. Use coins, leaves, or tagboard cutouts for embossing.

You can make your own paper in the kitchen or outdoors. Use a location where an electrical outlet is handy for the blender and a little messiness won't be a problem.

Once your paper is dry, you can write on it with markers or watercolors. Haiku poetry done with pen and ink looks very nice on homemade paper. Calligraphy is fun, too. (Special markers are available for calligraphic writing.)

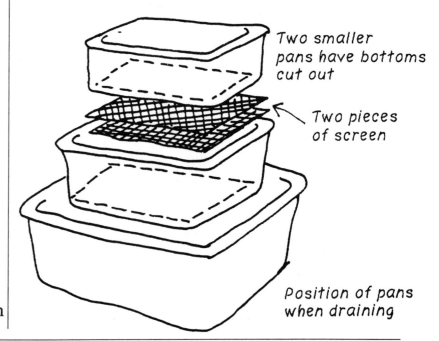

Two smaller pans have bottoms cut out

Two pieces of screen

Position of pans when draining

 ## MATERIALS

Narrow box, like a shoe box, with a lid

2 small mirrors

Masking tape

Scissors

Hot glue gun

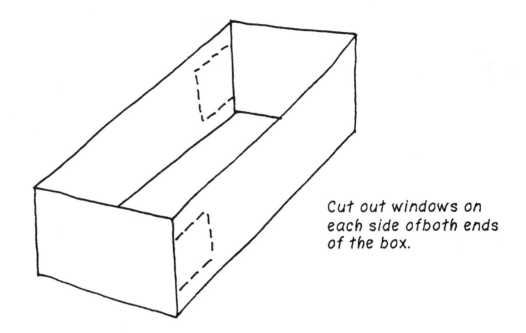

Cut out windows on each side of both ends of the box.

Using the mirrors as patterns, trace around them near the bottom of two sides of the box on opposite ends of the box, as shown in diagram. Cut the two sections out. Place the mirrors at an angle inside the box, opposite the cut out openings. Use tape to hold them in place. Adjust the mirrors until you can see out of the top hole by looking into the bottom hole. Use the hot glue gun to glue the mirrors in place along their edges.

Put the lid back on the box. Seal the lid to the box with masking tape.

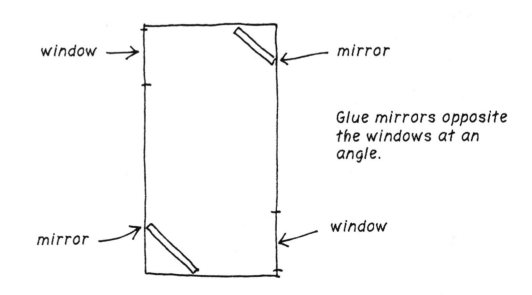

window →

← mirror

Glue mirrors opposite the windows at an angle.

mirror →

← window

ZANY BALLOON PEOPLE

These characters are all feet!

Balloon*

Felt-tip marking pens, washable-type (Permanent inks tend to break the balloon.)

Construction paper

Poster board or tagboard, 12" x 12"

Blow up the balloon, and knot the end.

Draw the pattern shown to create feet with shoes. If you want bare feet, draw on toes. Trace the pattern with tissue paper, then use that to draw the foot shape onto the tagboard. Cut the foot section from the posterboard. Cut slits as shown. Decorate the feet with markers as you desire. Shoe laces can be inserted into the tagboard by threading yarn through holes made with a paper punch. Insert the knotted end of the balloon into the feet, so the balloon person will stand up.

*See warning, page 69.

Now, decorate the balloon with markers to create facial features, hair, eyeglasses or whatever. Cut out ears, jewelry, or head bands from construction paper and glue in place.

Hair can be made by gluing sections of yarn on the balloon, or cutting long narrow strips of tissue paper, curling them around a pencil, and then gluing curls in place.

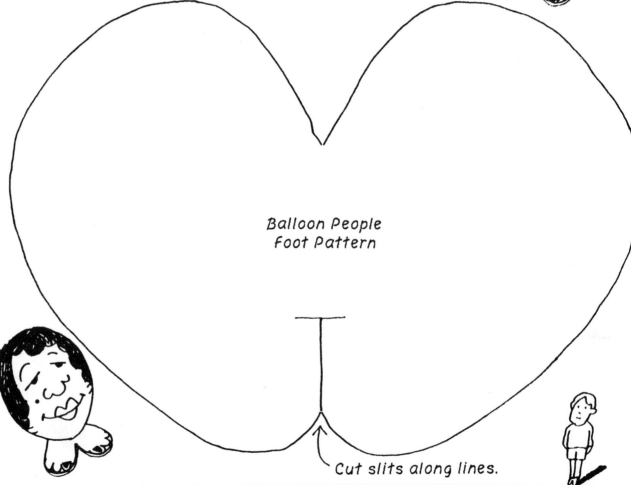

Balloon People
Foot Pattern

Cut slits along lines.

BIG MOUTH PUPPETS

✂ MATERIALS ✂

1 empty gelatin box for each puppet

1 sock

Scissors

Glue

Fabric scraps, pompoms, yarn, sequins, felt

Glue-on eyes: homemade or storebought

Tape

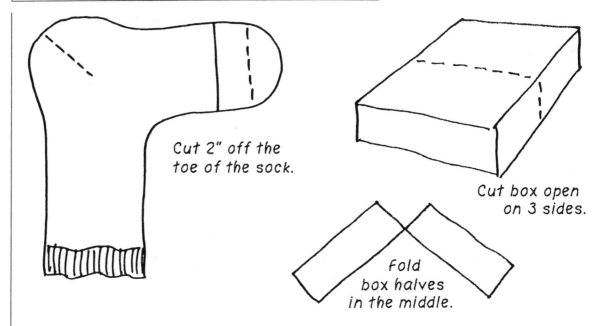

Cut 2" off the toe of the sock.

Cut box open on 3 sides.

Fold box halves in the middle.

Tape the open end of the gelatin box closed. Use scissors to cut across the middle and two sides of the box. Don't cut the other broad side. Fold the box in half along the uncut side. This box will be the puppet's mouth.

Cut across the toe of the sock, about 2" from the end. Slip the sock over the box so it creates a head and neck for the puppet. You may have to cut a larger opening in the sock to get it to fit over the box. Glue the sock to the box. Use the fabric scraps to cover the box, and then decorate both the box and sock, creating a character of your choice. Felt teeth can be glued inside the open mouth, and a red oval glued in place can be a tongue. Glue on the plastic eyes or make your own from felt scraps.

Bring the puppet to life by placing your arm inside the sock and your fingers in the box halves.

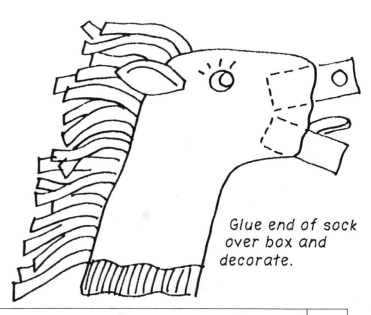

Glue end of sock over box and decorate.

 MATERIALS

Construction paper or tagboard,
9" x 12"

Crayons

Pencil

Scissors

Newspaper

Stapler

Take a good look at yourself. Look at your hairstyle, hair color, and clothing. Then draw yourself on the tagboard, and color in all details. Draw big, using the whole piece of paper. Make sure the arms and legs and neck are strong and thick.

Cut out. Trace your cut out figure on another piece of tagboard for the back of the puppet. Cut out. Color it like a back view of yourself. Staple or glue all around the edges, leaving the bottom open.

Make a newspaper stick by folding the paper in 1" folds, starting at a corner. Fold the paper and tape at the middle. Cut off the ends to even them up. Insert the end of the newspaper roll into the puppet, and staple or tape to secure.

For fun, make a whole family of puppets including your dog and cat!

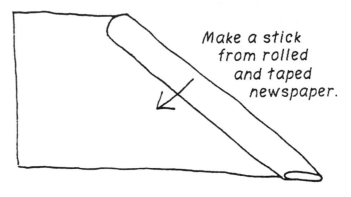

Make a stick from rolled and taped newspaper.

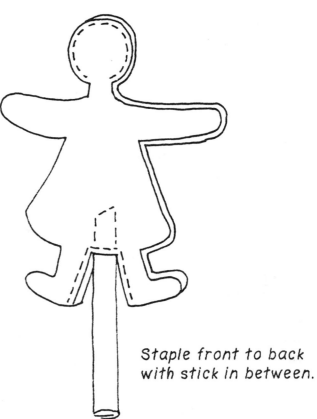

Staple front to back with stick in between.

Construction paper:
1 black, 1 white
(at least 12" x 18")

Chalk or white crayon

Projector

Scissors

Silhouettes are an old-fashioned form of portraiture. Work with a friend to create silhouettes. Set up a projector with no film in it. (You can shine a strong flashlight through a tissue paper roll.) Project the light onto a plain wall. Sit in front of the projector light so that the light shines on the side of your face. Your profile will project onto the wall behind you. Have your helper tape a piece of black construction paper to the wall. Then using white chalk or white crayon,

your helper should trace the outline of your profile onto the black paper.

When the tracing is finished, carefully cut your profile out and glue it to a larger piece of white paper.

Use the same method to create silhouettes of toys, plants, or an abstract that might create an interesting outline. Just set the objects on a table in front of the projector.

Some silhouettes can be made without using a bright light or projector. Draw action figures, scenes showing people and animals running, jumping, boxing, falling, or whatever. Don't worry about any details, just show the outlines of the figures. Draw on white paper and cut out along the outlines. Then trace onto black paper, using a pencil. Cut out carefully and glue to a larger piece of white paper.

Make a favorite photograph extra special by turning it into a free-standing piece of sculpture.

 MATERIALS

Photograph, enlarged to
8" x 10", if possible

Spray adhesive

Foam core board
(a lightweight foam board
available in art supply stores)

Craft knife

Two strips of wood molding, as
long as the picture's base

White glue

Scissors

Use scissors to carefully cut around the outline or outside edges of the photo's subject. Spray the back of the photo with the spray adhesive, and glue it to the foam core board. When the adhesive is dry, cut the foam board to fit the photo with a sharp craft knife. Cut by gently slicing around the outline until it is cut evenly. Leave a straight edge at the bottom of the photo. Paint or stain the wooden strips as desired. Glue the photo between the two strips of wood. They will form a base, enabling the photo sculpture to stand alone.

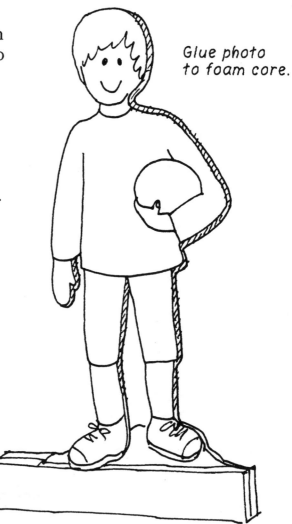

Glue photo
to foam core.

Glue wood strips
to front and back
of foam.

CUT-PAPER ART

Cut-Paper Mosaics

This project is good to use up all your scraps of colored paper. Tesserae (a big word for small pieces of paper) are used. They are strips of colored construction paper cut into ¹/₂" or ³/₄" pieces.

✄ MATERIALS ✄

Colored construction paper

Glue: dilute white glue with a little water or use paste or rubber cement.

Scissors

Construction paper, illustration board, tag board, or gift boxes to glue the tesserae onto

Small boxes to sort the tesserae

Cut the small pieces of construction paper, sorting them by colors into small containers or boxes. You can use a pencil to outline your design on the construction paper background, or begin by gluing tesserae onto the background. Fill in all areas with cut paper pieces, allowing some background to show if you wish.

Stop 1" from edge. →

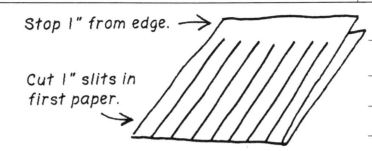

Cut 1" slits in first paper.

Trim 1" strips from second paper.

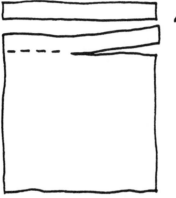

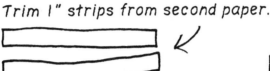

Weave a Picture

✄ MATERIALS ✄

Pictures cut from magazines

Scissors

Tape

Weave strips over and under slits.

Find two brightly colored pictures and trim them so they are the same size. Fold one picture in half horizontally. Starting at the fold, draw vertical lines about one inch apart, ending about an inch from the edge of the paper. Cut along the lines and open the picture flat.

On the second picture, draw horizontal lines about one inch apart. Cut one strip at a time from the second picture. Weave each strip into the first picture, which now serves as a paper "loom." Cut and weave one strip at a time, going over—then under—each paper strip. Make sure each strip is facing the same direction. Tape the edges in place as you go. When finished, you will have two pictures blended together, creating an interesting composition. Glue the woven picture onto a larger piece of colored construction paper if you wish.

Gold Medals

 MATERIALS

Jar lid to trace a circle

Notary seal (gold foil star emblems, found in stationery stores or made from aluminum foil)

30" length of ribbon: red, white or blue

Hole punch

Construction paper: red, white or blue

Fine-tip permanent marking pen

Trace a circle onto the construction paper using the jar lid as a template. Cut out. Moisten the back of the notary seal and stick it onto the circle, or glue a foil seal on. Punch a hole in the top of the paper circle and thread the length of ribbon through it. Knot the ends. With a marking pen, write whatever inscription you'd like (Best Sport) onto the gold emblem.

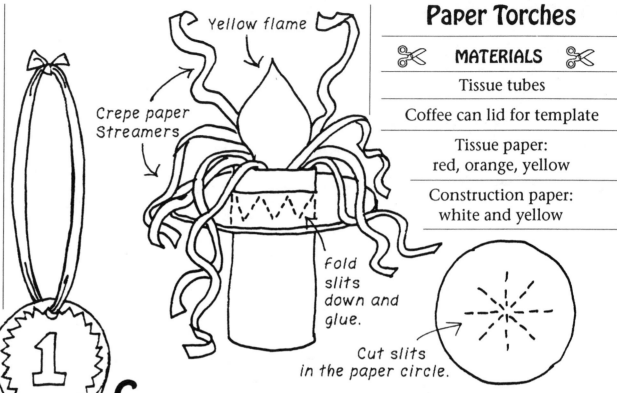

Yellow flame

Crepe paper Streamers

Fold slits down and glue.

Cut slits in the paper circle.

Paper Torches

MATERIALS

Tissue tubes

Coffee can lid for template

Tissue paper: red, orange, yellow

Construction paper: white and yellow

Cut a flame shape from the yellow paper. Cut and glue the white paper to cover the tube. Cut a large circle from the white paper (use a coffee can lid for a pattern). Cut two "x" shapes in the center, to create slits. Insert the covered tube through the slits. Push the paper circle down about one inch from the end of the tube, folding back the slits. Glue into place. Glue the yellow flame shape to the top end of the tube.

Cut strips of the colored tissue paper, about 12" long and ¼" wide. Glue them to the tube next to the flame shape.

Take off running with your torch, and the colored tissue will wave from the torch and appear to be flames.

A large torch can be created using tubes from gift wrap, a paper plate for the circle shape, and longer pieces of tissue paper.

✂ MATERIALS ✂

Brown paper grocery bags
White glue
Pencil
Paper plate
Scissors
Brown construction paper, 8"x 8"

Roll paper and glue.

Glue logs into place.

Cut the paper bags into 4"-wide strips. Cut the strips into 2¹/₂"-long pieces. To make a log, roll the strip around the pencil, and glue the cut end. Slide the cylinder off the pencil and repeat. When you have about 16 of these cylinders (logs) made, you are ready to construct the base of the cabin.

Arrange the logs on a paper plate, alternating the logs at the corners. Glue them together. Glue a second row of logs on top of the first, staggering them at the corners. Continue building upward until your cabin is four logs high.

Roll some smaller logs. Use two strips 3" x 2¹/₂" to make logs for the first row that will taper to the roof. Then make three more pairs of logs, with each pair getting a little shorter than the last. Glue them at opposite ends of the cabin. Glue longer ones on first and taper to the roofline.

Fold the brown construction paper in half, and adjust the size to fit your cabin. Glue it atop the logs.

You can use small pieces of the grocery bags or colored paper to create a chimney, windows, shutters, a porch step, or whatever details you choose.

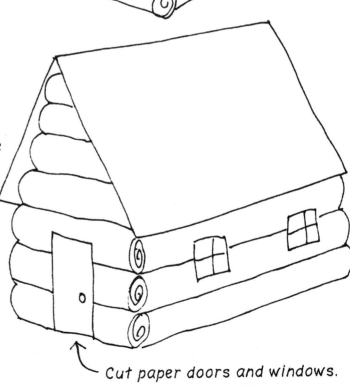

Cut paper doors and windows.

Wigwams

Paper coffee filters,
the flat-bottomed kind

Brown tempera paint or marker

Paint or color the outside of the filter. Cut a hole for a doorway. Wigwams were made from branches and grasses held together with mud. To make yours look more realistic, glue on bits of straw or cut paper.

Native American Indians lived in different kinds of houses, depending upon which tribe they belonged to and where they lived. Here are two types.

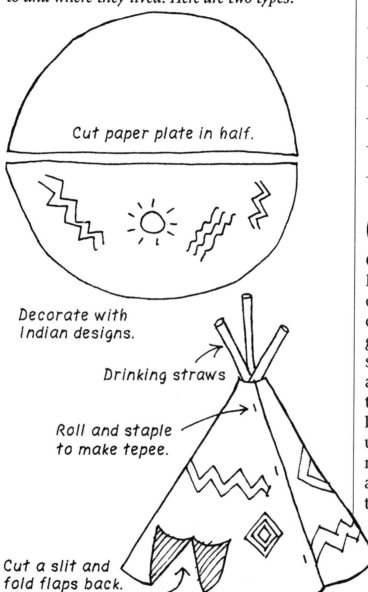

Cut paper plate in half.

Decorate with Indian designs.

Drinking straws

Roll and staple to make tepee.

Cut a slit and fold flaps back.

Tepees

✂ **MATERIALS** ✂

Paper plate

3 drinking straws

Marking pens or tempera paints

Staples

Scissors

Cut the paper plate in half. One half will make one tepee. Decorate the plate with Indian designs using colorful markers or paints. Roll the cut ends together to create a cone and staple. Trim a bit of the point away to insert drinking straws so they stick out of the top, to look like the lodge poles the Indians used to keep their houses upright. Cut a slit from the bottom and fold the edges back towards the tepee to create a door.

Cut out a wagon bed from brown paper. Cut slits as shown. Fold the sides up and glue. Cut out a top for the wagon from white paper. Glue the sides to the wagon, inside the wagon bed.

Cut out four wagon wheels from lightweight cardboard. Color with marking pens or paint. Glue to the sides of the wagon base. If you want movable wheels, you can use brads to fasten the wheels to the wagon, inserting the brads through the wheel's center and the wagon.

To create a wagon seat, cut a brown paper rectangle and fold. Glue in place. Punch two holes in the front of the wagon bed, and insert the yarn.

You can decorate the wagon with barrels made from rolls of paper, yarn ropes, and written messages, such as "California or Bust!"

Paper people and mules can be colored and cut out of construction paper or lightweight white cardboard. Make a wagon train, several wagons long, and bring them together in a circle at night.

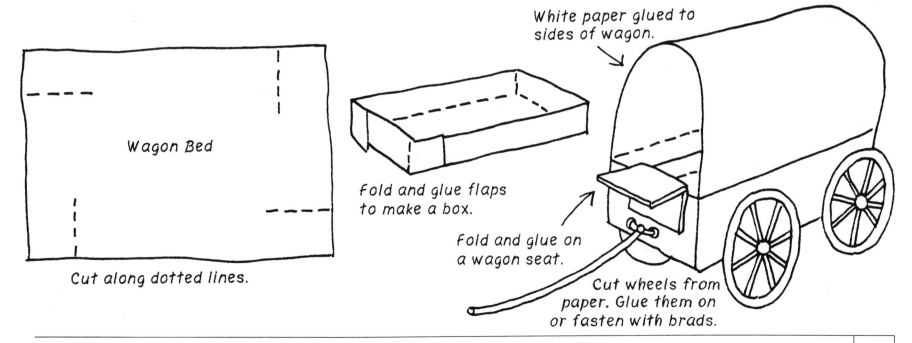

Wagon Bed

Cut along dotted lines.

Fold and glue flaps
to make a box.

White paper glued to
sides of wagon.

Fold and glue on
a wagon seat.

Cut wheels from
paper. Glue them on
or fasten with brads.

 MATERIALS

Brown paper grocery bag

Marking pens of assorted colors

The Indians in the west didn't write to each other with quill pens. They used hides and homemade dyes to communicate their important thoughts. Winter counts were an important part of Indian life. A winter count was made on a large tanned animal hide. Each year important events were drawn on the hide. These records showed what had happened over several winters' time. They were handed down through the years and are a valuable record of life in those days.

You can make your winter count from a grocery bag. Cut the bag apart at the seams, and smooth it out flat. Tear all the edges away, giving the bag a rough shape, like an animal skin.

Using the marking pens, draw events in your life. Start with your birth and record all the important things that have happened to you by drawing pictures to represent each event. It's easy to show family births, moves, new schools, and hobbies. Or, imagine you are a young Indian and draw a winter count of your life.

To store your winter count, roll it up and tie with a piece of yarn.

ROLLED PAPER BEADS

✂ MATERIALS ✂

Colored pages from magazines

Pencil

White glue

String

You may want to wear a color-ful bead necklace as you write your winter count.

Cut triangle shapes from some magazine pages. Small triangles make smaller beads, larger triangles make larger beads. Experiment a little, trying several sizes to make your neck-lace interesting.

Roll the paper triangle over a pencil with the wide end down first. As the point rolls up over the broad side of the paper, rub a little glue under the pointed end. Roll tight. Hold it firmly for a few seconds, to be sure the glue will stick. Then slide the bead off the pencil.

Make a pile of beads; then begin stringing them on the string. Colorful yarn looks fine; dental floss is very sturdy. Tie a knot with the ends and wear with pride!

Cut triangles from magazine pages.

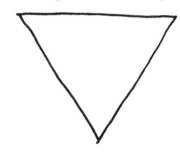

Roll up and glue.

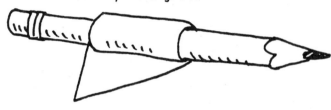

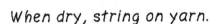

When dry, string on yarn.

SILVER & TURQUOISE INDIAN BRACELETS

 MATERIALS

Aluminum foil

Empty toilet tissue tube

Small sea shell macaroni

Blue food coloring

White glue

Scissors

Rubbing alcohol or water

Indians in the southwest love to make and wear beautiful silver and turquoise jewelry. You can, too!

Using scissors, cut the toilet tissue tube apart down one side. Then, cut off a section about 1½" wide. Trim the corners so they are slightly rounded as shown.

Using a strip of aluminum foil twice as big as the section of paper tube, cover the tube section with the foil, shiny side out. Smooth the foil and press the edges to the inside of the tube section. This is your silver bracelet.

Now, color the macaroni to represent turquoise stones found in the desert of the southwest. Fill a cup with ½ cup of rubbing alcohol. (Alcohol dries and evaporates more quickly than water, but you can use water.) Tint the alcohol with several drops of blue food coloring. Drop macaroni sea shells into the alcohol, and let them set until they are dyed a bright blue. This takes about 10 minutes. Place the macaroni on a plate and let dry.

When the "stones" are dry, glue them onto the bracelet with dabs of white glue. Make any designs you wish.

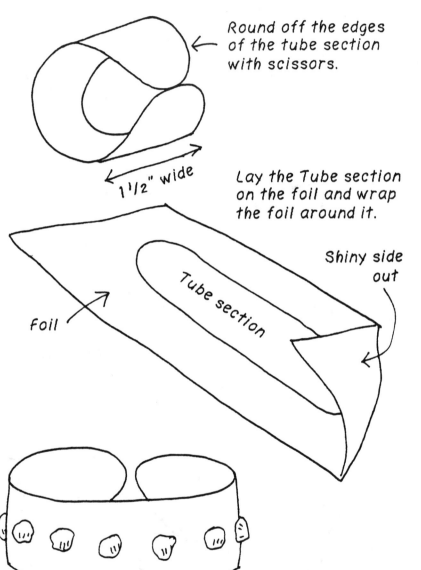

Round off the edges of the tube section with scissors.

1½" wide

Lay the Tube section on the foil and wrap the foil around it.

Shiny side out

Foil

Tube section

Glue the turquoise "stones" in place.

CLAY & DOUGH

Working with Ceramic Clays

Clay is such a great medium—it's not expensive, not too messy, and takes few supplies. Children of all ages love to work with it. Projects turn out so shiny and "real." Best of all, it's a very expressive medium; most children derive real satisfaction from both the process and the end result. An added benefit is that pinch pots and other ceramics make great paper clip holders or tiny vases for a bouquet of violets. Imagine how pleased a young potter will be to see his or her work of art being used and displayed!

Pottery clay can be purchased at art supply stores, some paint stores, and through any ceramic shop. It costs about $4.00 for 25 pounds. Twenty-five pounds makes about 50 small dishes or pots. The clay will need to be fired if you want the pottery to be permanent. In order to adequately fire it at the necessary temperature, you will have to use a kiln. While few of us have ready access to a kiln, most local ceramic shops will fire projects for you, charging a few cents for each piece fired. Be sure to make firing arrangements before you buy your clay.

There are three ways to build pots or dishes from clay. *Slab, coil-built* and *pinch* are easy enough for children of all ages to do. The secret of a successful clay piece is to "pull" the piece into shape, using the tips of your fingers to shape. Avoid patching small pieces of clay together. Also, be careful that you don't pinch the edges of your object so thin that it cracks while drying or firing.

Drying and Firing

No matter what type of clay project you do, you must allow the finished item to dry thoroughly. This can take at least a week to ten days. Test for dryness by holding the pot to your cheek. If it feels cold, it is not completely dry.

If you fire clay items that aren't dry inside, the high temperatures of firing cause the internal clay molecules to explode. If your pot explodes during firing, not only will that pot be ruined, but the flying bits of pottery within the kiln will break other items being fired and can cause serious damage to the inside of the kiln. Don't be overanxious to get something fired. You can hurry drying time along by placing the items in a warm spot, like near a stove, on top of a water heater, or near a heating vent. Direct sunlight will dry the items, but if it's too hot, they may dry too fast and crack.

Finishes

One advantage in using fired clay is the variety of finishing techniques and effects that can be used on the finished object.

The most permanent finish is a ceramic glaze specially formulated to be fired in the kiln. These glazes come in a wide variety of colors and effects, from opaque to transparent. The glaze is painted with a paintbrush on the fired clay object, allowed to dry, and then fired again in the kiln. This sets the glaze permanently, so ceramic dishes hold water and can even be washed in the dishwasher. Never apply glaze to the bottom of a ceramic piece as the glaze will melt the piece to the kiln. In fact, always carefully wipe the bottom edge before firing a glazed piece. Always specify that you want lead-free glaze, safe for eating utensils, when purchasing glaze. These firing glazes can be purchased through any ceramic shop. Costs vary from $1.00 to $3.00 per jar. Glazes are applied with regular paintbrushes and clean up is with soap and water.

While glazing is very popular, there are many other ways to finish a fired ceramic piece. Acrylic paints and finishes, sold in art supply stores, work very well. Although they don't need to be fired, they do dry to a waterproof finish. Watercolors and tempera paints can also be brushed on. They will be permanent if the piece is then sprayed with an acrylic spray finish.

One of my favorite techniques for finishing clay pieces is using a soft cloth to rub paste shoe polish over the surface of the clay. It gives the pot a weathered effect and is particularly nice with textured clay surfaces. Use it to finish clay "fossils." This method is inexpensive, quick and easy to do. When the polish is dry, brush on a coat or two of acrylic floor wax. It will dry to a nice soft sheen. Advantages to using the floor wax include its low cost, availability, and easy clean-up with soap and water. A disadvantage is that it isn't permanent. The finished piece can't be washed again and again. But it is a fine finish to use for clay items that will be displayed such as plaques, paperweights or sculptures.

A slightly messy finishing method involves painting the fired clay pieces with tempera, drying them, and then dipping the pieces into melted wax. Using a double-boiler to melt paraffin, lower the clay piece into the hot wax with a wire strainer. Lift it out gently, letting excess wax drip off. Cool the ceramic piece on a plate covered with waxed paper. When cool, it will have a nice sheen. Adults must do this part of the process because the wax can ignite at high temperatures. Waxed pieces are very nice to use as Christmas ornaments or display pieces.

Chalking can be done to a finished fired piece. It creates a soft, delicate effect. The fired piece is given a coat of white acrylic paint. When dry, apply chalk pastels with a bristle brush. Scrub the bristles into the chalk and then apply to the desired areas on the clay piece. This technique is used to create natural looking animal and wildlife sculptures. Once the chalk is applied, give the piece a spray coating of acrylic low-sheen finish.

Perfect Pinch Pots

Take a ball of clay the size of a large orange. Shape it into a pot by first pushing both thumbs together into the middle and shaping it by pulling the sides out from the center. Don't pinch the edges too thin. Build it up and out from the center, giving it the shape you want.

Wet your fingertips in a little water and smooth out any cracks in the surface of the pot.

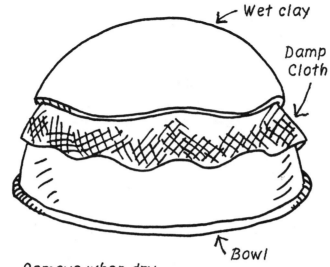

Wet clay

Damp Cloth

Bowl

Remove when dry.

Simple Slab Dish

A very easy clay dish can be made using the slab method. Use a rolling pin or large wooden dowel to roll the clay out flat and smooth—just like making sugar cookies! Roll the clay out to 1/2" thick. Cut a large shape from the slab; a large free-form oval is just fine. Place a damp cloth over a form or mold such as a bowl. Drape the wet clay over it to dry. Allow the clay to dry over the form, and it will retain the molded shape after firing. Most bowls found in the kitchen work very well. You can drape the clay over the upturned base of the bowl as shown or you can place the damp cloth inside the bowl, and lay the clay on the inside bottom of the bowl. It might take about a week for the clay to dry on the form before finishing and firing.

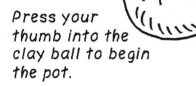

Press your thumb into the clay ball to begin the pot.

Smooth any cracks on the pot.

Roll out clay to about 1/2" thick.

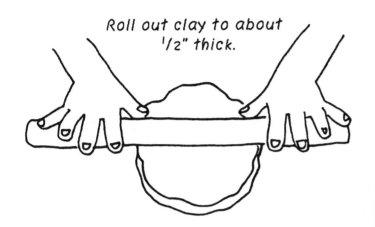

After you have tried the simple slab dish, or if you are pretty confident of your clay handling ability, you can try cutting slab projects out and pressing them into a variety of shapes. Depending upon the shape of your base, you can make rectangular dishes or round ones, ovals or squares.

Here's how to do one to get you started. Roll the clay to about 1/2" thick. Use a table knife to cut a 4" x 4" rectangle. This will be the base of your dish. Cut four sides, each 2" x 4". If you cut out a paper pattern first, you will be sure to have all sides equal.

Join the sides to the base by scoring the edges. Scrape the clay edges with a table knife to rough them up a bit. Moisten the scored edges with a little water and press the edges together. Roll a long, thin clay coil (about the size of a large earthworm) and press it along the inside seam where the edges meet, especially around the corners. Smooth it down with a Popsicle stick or similar tool.

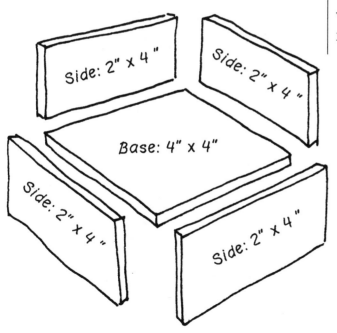

Side: 2" x 4"
Side: 2" x 4"
Base: 4" x 4"
Side: 2" x 4"
Side: 2" x 4"

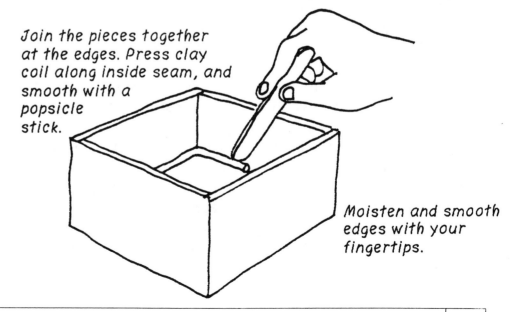

Join the pieces together at the edges. Press clay coil along inside seam, and smooth with a popsicle stick.

Moisten and smooth edges with your fingertips.

COILED POTTERY CREATIONS

Coiled pottery is more sophisticated than slab methods. People throughout history have used the coil method to create beautiful, durable containers.

To get started, make a base by flattening a slab of clay to about 1/2" thick. Cut out a round shape from the slab, tracing from a pattern such as a glass or a coffee can with a table knife. Now make several coils by rolling the clay between the palms of both hands, creating a smooth rope of clay. Make each coil about 1/2" thick and 12" long.

Score the edges of the base with a table fork. Dip a sponge in water and rub over the scoring to moisten it. Place a coil on the top edge of the base and pinch one end flat to the base, so that the coil is joined firmly to the pot base. Continue adding coils atop one another, scoring and sponging each coil's surface before winding another above it.

When a coil has been used up, make a diagonal cut at the end of it. Do the opposite to the new coil. Splice them together by scoring, sponging and applying finger pressure.

When your pot is the size and shape you want, pinch off the end of the last coil, and using some water and finger pressure, blend the end into the rest of the pot. Continue smoothing the surface of the pot with finger pressure and slight moisture. If you want your pot to hold water, you need to sponge and use finger pressure to smooth the coils together.

Special effects can be created on the surface of your pot by pressing objects into the smooth, wet clay to create textures and repeated patterns. Look for odds and ends such as macaroni, nuts and bolts, bits of heavy lace, pieces of burlap or whatever you can find.

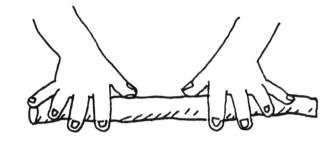

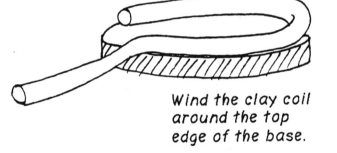

Wind the clay coil around the top edge of the base.

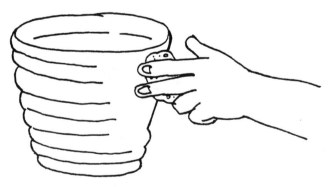

Use a moist sponge and fingertips to smooth the coils flat.

MAKE YOUR OWN FOSSILS

★ MATERIALS ★

Soft clay

Imprinting items such as leaves, pebbles, shells

Shoe polish

Acrylic finish

Dinosaur enthusiasts love creating "fossils" from natural objects. Find a few leaves, pebbles, sea shells, or even dead bugs for imprinting. Use any kind of soft clay. Your fossils can be air-dried or fired in the kiln.

Roll the clay into a smooth ball; then press it flat on the table top. Use a little water to smooth around the outside edges of the clay. Press your chosen object directly into the clay. Then remove it. It's imprint will remain. If you are satisfied with the quality of the imprint, allow it to dry. If not, roll the clay up and try again.

When the fossil is dry, finish it by rubbing brown shoe polish gently over the surface. Let the shoe polish dry and then brush on a coat of clear acrylic finish or acrylic floor wax, or spray with a clear acrylic spray finish.

Press a leaf into the soft clay.
Then gently lift it out.

Use leaves, shells or whatever you find to create fossils.

★ **MATERIALS** ★

Clay

Table knife

Straw or pencil

Toothpicks

Newspaper

Glaze, paint or shoe polish

Dried flowers

Ribbon or yarn

Weed pockets are easy to make and nice to give as a gift. Roll a slab of clay out to about ¼" thickness. Use a toothpick or pencil to trace an outline on the slab and a table knife to cut it out. Cut a rectangle from the clay about 5" wide and 9" long. Cut off the corners from one end, creating a rounded edge as shown. Use a drinking straw or a pencil to punch a hole in the rounded end. Moisten the edges of the clay and fold the bottom third of the rectangle up over itself to create a pocket. Press the edges together to seal the clay. Decorate the surface by drawing simple designs or patterns with toothpicks or by pressing pieces of burlap or lace gently into the clay.

Insert a piece of crumpled newspaper into the pocket to keep it open as the piece dries. When completely dry, remove the paper and fire in a kiln. Weed pockets can be glazed, painted, or finished with shoe polish. Stick some dried flowers, weeds or pods into the pocket. Hang on the wall by the hole, or string some ribbon or yarn through the hole, tie a bow, and hang from the ribbon.

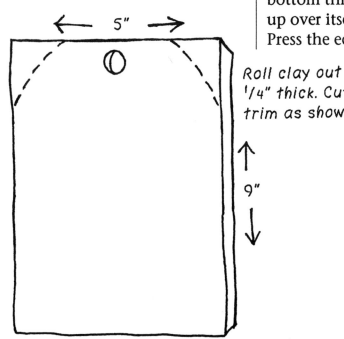

← 5" →

9"

Roll clay out ¼" thick. Cut and trim as shown.

Fold up to make a pocket.

Press edges together.

After firing, fill with dried weeds and hang from a ribbon.

★ MATERIALS ★

Clay
Gingerbread boy cookie cutter
Toothpicks
Small bowl
Glaze

Roll some clay flat, to about ¼" thickness. Use a gingerbread boy cookie cutter, or trace around a pattern with a toothpick. Cut out with a table knife. Moisten your fingertips and smooth the cut edges slightly.

Use toothpicks to make eyes, a smile, and buttons in the clay. You can also roll tiny balls of clay, moistening slightly, and press into the surface of the boy to create buttons or decorative trim.

Lay the cut-out gingerbread boy inside a paper bowl or salad bowl to dry. This gives the clay a concave shape, perfect for a spoon rest. When completely dry, fire in a kiln. Finish the piece with a glossy glaze of your choice and fire.

Hair Barrettes

★ MATERIALS ★

Leftover clay

Metal barrettes

Imprinting materials such as nuts, macaroni, buttons

Glaze or paint

Glue

These simple and very special hair barrettes are made from small leftover clay scraps. Use purchased metal barrettes for mounting. Cut or roll the clay into rectangular pieces slightly larger than the metal barrette base. Incise a decorative design on the clay using toothpicks to draw with or nuts, macaroni, or buttons to make prints and patterns. Place the decorated clay piece on a slightly curved surface, such as the underside of an up-turned plate. Let dry. Fire if you choose. Paint or glaze, and glue to the back of the metal barrette. I use a hot glue gun for this project, but any reliable craft glue works.

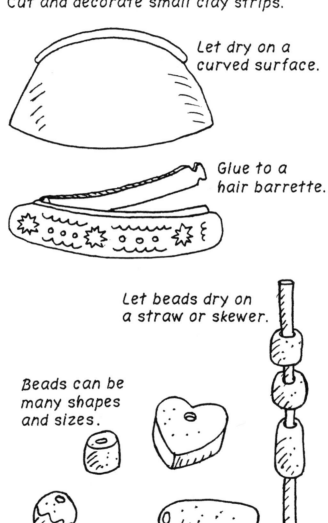

Cut and decorate small clay strips.

Let dry on a curved surface.

Glue to a hair barrette.

Let beads dry on a straw or skewer.

Beads can be many shapes and sizes.

Beads

★ MATERIALS ★

Leftover clay

Straws or bolts

Glaze or paints

Acrylic finish

Thread or floss

You can make great beads from your leftover clay scraps. Make them large or small, in any shapes you choose. Stick a drinking straw or long, wide bolt through the middle of each bead, allowing several to dry in place on a straw. If you want a smaller hole in the middle, stick them on a barbecue skewer or nail.

When dry, the beads can be fired or not, as you choose. Decorate with paint, glaze, or leave them natural. Spray with an acrylic finish. String them on skinny ropes, ribbons, dental floss or fishing line.

★ MATERIALS ★

Clay

Toothpicks

Glaze

Buttons made from clay look great on sweaters, coats—almost anything you want to personalize.

Either roll clay into a thin slab and cut out the button shapes, or roll into small balls in your hand and flatten against the table top. Use toothpicks or narrow skewers to punch holes (at least two) in the middle of the buttons.

Use toothpicks to press in a surface design. If you have access to leatherworking tools, tiny designs can be imprinted.

Let the buttons dry, and then fire them. To finish, spray with acrylic or glaze the top surface and fire. Be careful to keep glaze from getting on the underside or the glaze will melt in the kiln and fire the buttons

to the kiln's shelf. When fired and glazed, buttons made from ceramic clay can be machine washed and dried, on the gentle cycle. It's best to button the garment and turn it inside out first. Keep in mind that clay shrinks when drying and firing. If you are creating a button to fit a particular size buttonhole, make it about $^1/_3$ larger than needed to allow for shrinkage.

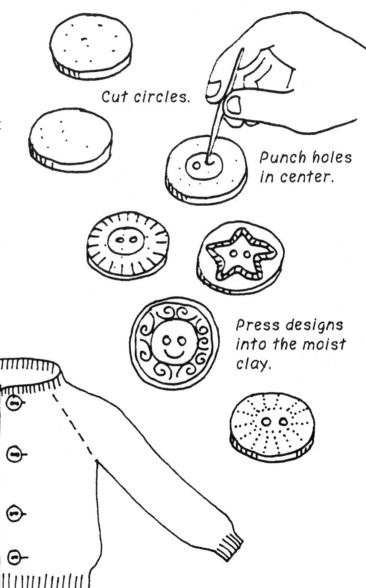

Cut circles.

Punch holes in center.

Press designs into the moist clay.

Sew buttons on to your favorite clothes.

Sawdust Clay

²/₃ parts fine sawdust
(any kind except redwood)

¹/₃ part flour

Water

Large bowl or bucket

Wooden spoon

Ceramic and pottery clays are lots of fun, but you aren't limited to them. There are several kinds of clay and dough you can create yourself from inexpensive materials.

Few people have used this type of clay, but after I tried it, I loved it! It's very inexpensive, and the results can be quite impressive. When dried in the sun, sawdust clay becomes very hard and can be sanded with sandpaper before it's painted. Children of all ages can use it, clean up is easy, and one bucket of sawdust will keep you busy for a long time.

To mix the clay, use a large bowl or bucket. Mix ²/₃ parts of sawdust and ¹/₃ part of flour together. Pour in water and mix until it reaches a stiff but "squishy" consistency. Add

more flour if it is too crumbly. The clay needs some kneading before the gluten in the flour becomes elastic, holding the sawdust together. Work it in your hands or on a table top covered with newspapers. Play with the clay a little until it becomes easy to shape.

This clay has a thick heavy texture, and the best type of projects seem to be "Indian"-type pottery pieces. Take large balls of clay. Push your thumbs together into the center, shaping the sides as you go for bowls and other containers. Sawdust clay can also be rolled flat and cut into shapes with cookie cutters. Poke a hole in each cut-out with a drinking straw. When dry, string with yarn to make simple wall decorations or Christmas tree ornaments.

This clay air-dries very hard. It should be placed directly in the sun, if possible. When dry,

you can sand it or not, depending upon what you like. Use tempera or acrylic paints to decorate the finished objects. To give your pieces a glossy coating, spray with acrylic clear finish or paint with acrylic floor wax.

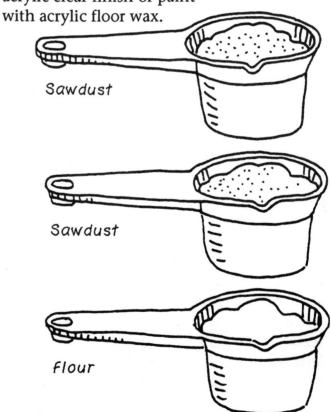

Sawdust

Sawdust

Flour

Bread Clay

★ MATERIALS ★

Dry, stale white bread

White glue

This clay is nice for making small, delicate ornaments and figurines. You can also make flowers, forming each petal by rolling and pressing the clay into shape.

To create bread clay, remove the bread crusts and break the bread into small pieces. Add the glue, one tablespoon of white glue per one slice of bread. Mix with a spoon, then knead with your fingers until it's soft and pliable. If you want to work with a colored dough, add a small amount of tempera paint to the clay. Knead it to spread the color evenly. This clay can also be tinted by mixing food coloring with the white glue before mixing with the bread.

To detail the clay figures, use your fingernails or toothpicks. When the figurines are finished, glaze with a mixture of equal parts of water and white glue to prevent cracking or shrinking as the clay dries. After the pieces are air-dried, they can be painted with acrylics, tempera or given a rubbed finish with paste shoe polish.

This clay keeps several days in the refrigerator, if well sealed.

Salt Dough

There are many recipes for salt dough. Some require cooking, some don't. Some have a stiffer texture, just right for creating small details. Others are softer, ideal for young hands. All are inexpensive and store well when wrapped tightly or in an airtight container in the refrigerator. Salt dough can also be frozen and thawed for use later.

Food coloring is usually recommended to color the various doughs. Liquid or powder tempera paint also works. If you use plenty of coloring, you don't have to paint the surface of the finished object. Simply spray it with clear acrylic sealer. Brightly colored dough looks better than faded, weaker colors once the dough dries. Paste food coloring sold with cake decorating sup-plies gives a more intense color, so you may choose to use that instead of the liquid variety.

Use waxed paper as a working surface and also to air-dry dough products. Work on foil-covered cookie sheets for projects that must be baked in the oven.

If you are making a hanging ornament, small pieces of twisted wire or paper clips can be inserted into the dough before it hardens. Otherwise, remember to make a hole with a straw or nail before the dough hardens.

Salt dough is good for molding. Use gelatin molds, candy molds or marzipan molds. Dust the mold's surface lightly with cornstarch or flour before pressing dough in place.

A variety of tools can be used with salt dough. Search your garage tool box and kitchen

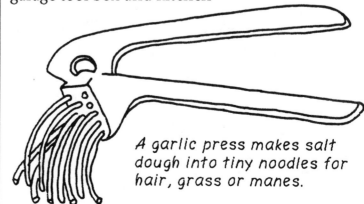

A garlic press makes salt dough into tiny noodles for hair, grass or manes.

drawers for picks, nails, Popsicle sticks, bottle caps, tweezers, golf tees, and cookie cutters. Melon ball cutters and pastry wheels are also useful. The most fun and versatile tool is a garlic press. Use it to squeeze out tiny noodles of dough to create hair, beards, grass or manes. Inexpensive garlic presses can be found in a supermarket or kitchen store.

Salt Dough 1

★   MATERIALS   ★

2 cups cornstarch
4 cups baking soda
2$\frac{1}{2}$ cups cold water

Measure the cornstarch and baking soda into a pot. Mix and add 2$\frac{1}{2}$ cups of cold water. Place on medium heat. Stir for about 5 minutes, until the mixture thickens. Remove from the heat. Cover the pot with a wet paper towel. When cool, knead for about 5 minutes, working on a surface covered with waxed paper.

Allow objects to air-dry before painting.

Salt Dough 2

★   MATERIALS   ★

2$\frac{1}{4}$ cups water
2 cups salt
3 cups white flour
1 cup whole wheat flour

Bring the water to a boil in a saucepan. Remove from the heat and stir in the salt. Mix the flours together in a large bowl. Add the salt water to the flours and stir. Knead on a flour-covered surface.

Bake finished objects on a cookie sheet at 250° F for 2 to 3 hours. Check your objects every 20 minutes after the first 2 hours of baking.

When cool, decorate with tempera, acrylic or colored marking pens. Spray with clear acrylic finish to protect and preserve.

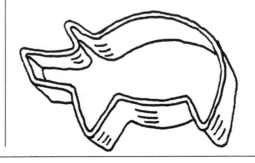

Salt Dough 3

This recipe resembles edible dough when baked. It puffs up slightly, softening edges and details. When baked, it is a soft light-brown color. Seal it with a clear matte finish, and you can make a loaf of bread that looks good enough to eat! This dough does not keep well, however, so use it as soon as it's made.

★   MATERIALS   ★

4 cups flour
1 cup salt
1$\frac{1}{2}$ cups warm water

Mix the flour and salt in a large bowl. Add warm water slowly, using your hands to mix all together. Wear rubber gloves if you wish, as the salt tends to dry your skin. Knead on a flour-covered surface for about 10 minutes, until the surface is smooth and elastic. Wrap the dough tightly or place in a covered container. Take out only what you will be using.

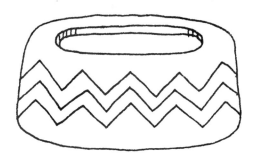

If you are making a large object, avoid having dough several inches thick as it will not cook evenly. You can build an armature to support a project by crumpling aluminum foil and building up your dough over it.

Bake thin objects about 30 minutes at 350° F. Larger objects require an hour or more, so set the oven at 300° F or 325° F. Cover any areas which brown before the object is completely baked with pieces of aluminum foil to prevent darkening.

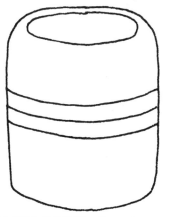

Salt Dough 4

This recipe makes my all-time favorite modeling clay. It is very much like the store-bought dough, but much cheaper and lots of fun to make.

★   **MATERIALS**   ★

1 cup flour

1 tablespoon salad oil

1 cup water

$1/2$ cup salt

2 teaspoons cream of tartar

Food coloring

Combine all ingredients in a large saucepan. Use a wooden spoon to stir over medium heat. Stir constantly to prevent sticking. The mixture will be soupy for several minutes and then suddenly it will stick together and can be stirred into a ball. When it thickens, remove from heat and continue stirring. Turn the hot ball out onto a floured surface, and begin kneading as it cools.

This recipe makes nice soft dough that can be colored brightly with food colors. It keeps in the refrigerator or freezer in a covered container. Use it to play around with or to make small objects which can be air-dried until hard. When dry they can be painted and sprayed with an acrylic sealer.

Salt Dough 5

★   **MATERIALS**   ★

1 cup salt

$1/2$ cup cornstarch

$3/4$ cup cold water

Stir all ingredients together over low heat. Stir constantly to prevent burning. In 2 or 3 minutes it will thicken and can no longer be stirred. Turn out onto waxed paper or aluminum foil and cool. When cool, knead until smooth. If the dough dries out, add some water. This recipe makes nice ornaments that are rolled and cut with cookie cutters or designed freehand. Allow to air-dry.

NUTSHELL ORNAMENTS

★ MATERIALS ★

Salt dough #3

Walnut shells

Toothpicks

Paper clips

Acrylic spray

Use the recipe for salt dough #3. This dough doesn't keep well, so only make the amount you plan to use in one session. You need a half of a walnut shell for each ornament or doll house creature. Pinch small bits of dough to create a sleeping mouse, baby, or any creature you like.

First, fill the shell with a ball of dough. Then moisten and press a tiny head to the ball in the shell. Create facial features with a toothpick. For a blanket, place a thin piece of dough across the shell and tuck in at the edges. Insert a paper clip or small piece of bent wire into the top of the head for hanging or leave as is for a small treasure. Cover the walnut shell with a small piece of aluminum foil, so it won't brown in the oven. Bake at 225° F for about 4 hours. Cool and paint with acrylic or tempera paints if you wish. Seal with an acrylic spray coating.

Clay Tablets

★ MATERIALS ★

Salt clay dough (not #3)

Rolling pin

Pasta letters

Toothpicks

Watercolors or shoe polish

Acrylic sealer

This project copies ancient clay tablets that were inscribed with sharp tools. The ancient cuneiform characters of the Assyrians are an example. This project is also a lot of fun for religious school classes, as the tablets given to Moses on Mount Sinai can be duplicated.

Use any of the salt clay recipes, except #3. Roll a ball of dough out flat with a rolling pin, and cut it into your tablet shape. Press letters into the surface to create your message. Small toy letters can be purchased in toy departments and are good for small hands to use. Older chil-

dren can use the alphabet pasta found in grocery stores. Use a toothpick tip to lift the pasta up from the clay after printing. Children may want to draw a picture story or use letters from the Greek or Hebraic alphabets.

Depending upon your recipe, air-dry or oven-bake the tablets. Finish with a light wash of watercolor paint or rub on a little shoe polish. Spray with an acrylic sealer. If you like, glue the tablets to a stained piece of wood and hang on the wall.

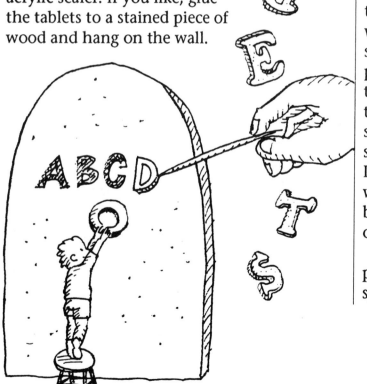

Alphabet Letters

★ MATERIALS ★

Salt dough

Thin wire

Colorful letters can be made and hung on a bedroom wall. Use any of the baked salt clay recipes. Roll the dough into thick ropes and shape into letters to spell out a special name or word. Moisten edges with water so they stick together when pressed into letter shapes. Tiny teddy bears, fruits and vegetables, or faces can be rolled and shaped from the dough and stuck into position on the letters. Insert a twisted piece of thin wire into the back of each letter before baking, so it can be hung on the wall.

After baking and cooling, paint with acrylic paints and spray with a glossy acrylic finish.

It's really fun to create a plate or basket full of fruits, vegetables and other foods. Glue the food in place on a paper plate to display as a work of art called a still life, or glue magnets to the backs of the individual pieces to use on your refrigerator. Larger pieces can be made to fill a basket or bowl.

Use any of the salt dough recipes. Color the dough with lots of food coloring so the food will be bright and appealing. Keep each clump of colored dough in a separate container or bag. Two colors can be kneaded together to create another color.

There's no limit to the variety of foods that you can create. I've listed some here, but look in your refrigerator for more ideas!

Cherry pie

Roll and cut two triangles from light tan dough. Roll several small balls from bright red dough. Moisten the balls slightly with water, and place them on top of one triangle. Be sure they are lined up along the edges. Lay the other triangle on top, creating the top crust of your piece of pie. Crimp the edges together at the wide end of the triangle to simulate a pinched crust. Use your fingers and a bit of water to moisten the edges so they stick together. With a toothpick, prick a few holes in the top of the crust.

Peas in a pod

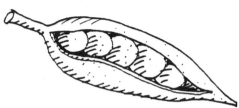

Roll and cut two flat fish-like shapes to create the pods. Roll nine small pea-shaped balls, and moisten each with a little water. Lay five atop one pod, and four atop the other. Press the edges of each pod up along the sides to hold the peas in place. Pinch a curved piece and attach as a stem. Press the two pods together at the top, moistening slightly so they stick together.

Bananas

Using yellow dough, roll cylindrical shapes between your palms. Taper both ends and chop the tips off with a sharp knife, so they are blunt. When the banana is dry, detail it with brown felt-tip markers. Bananas look best in bunches. Use a little water and pinch them together at the stems so they form a bunch.

Fried egg

Roll some white dough out flat, cutting a free-form shape from it for your egg white. Smooth the cut edge with a moistened finger tip, so it is rounded. Roll a ball from bright yellow dough to make the egg yolk. Press it lightly against the tabletop to flatten its base. Moisten the base of the yolk, and set it on top of the white.

Carrot

Using bright orange dough, roll a short fat cylinder for each carrot. By rolling the dough between your palms you can create a realistic carrot shape that is wide at the top and tapers to a narrow tip. With a paring knife, score the carrot in a few places to resemble the lines on carrots. To add a carrot top, press some bright green dough through a garlic press, moisten slightly and attach atop each carrot. Carrots look best in bunches of three. Moisten the sides of each so they stick together when dry.

Apple

Using bright red or yellow-green dough, roll a ball into an apple shape. Push in slightly at the bottom and insert a clove, if you have one, to resemble the stem at the base of an apple. Roll a tiny bit of brown dough and insert at the top for a stem. You may be able to use another clove as a top stem, depending upon the size of your apple. Is that a worm poking out of a hole in the side of the apple? Make the worm by rolling a tiny rope of white dough or pressing dough through a garlic press. Push a hole in the side of the apple with a skewer or pencil and insert the worm. Moisten the worm slightly so it will stick to the apple. When dry, use a black felt-tip marking pen to dot tiny eyes on the worm.

Pasta

There are two ways to create a dish of pasta—and don't forget, pasta comes in shades of green and red nowadays. If you want it to look like hand-made pasta, roll out some dough to about $1/8$" thickness. Use a sharp kitchen knife to slice narrow ribbons. Pile the noodles in a dish. If you want a narrower, finer type of pasta, press the dough through your garlic press. For either type, top with a large pat of butter made by rolling yellow dough out and cutting a patty-shape square from it. Moisten the underside of the butter patty and press atop the dish of pasta.

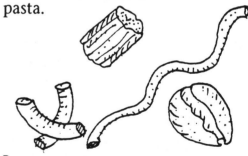

Don't stop now! Go ahead and roll tiny clusters of grapes, radishes, and lemons. Roll and cut out pieces to create artichokes, tacos, and french fries. Just be sure to allow each piece to air-dry or bake as needed. Then spray with a shiny coat of acrylic sealer.

★ **MATERIALS** ★

Salt dough #4,
tinted bright yellow-green

Uncooked spaghetti
(long thin noodles)

Aluminum foil (tear one 10"
piece for each cactus)

Dinner fork

Paper plate base to work on and
to display the cactus on

Crush foil to create base.

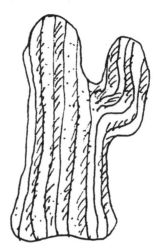

Press in ribs
with a fork.

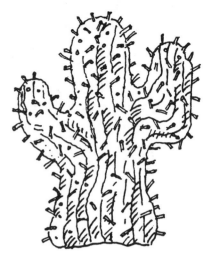

Stick broken spaghetti in
cactus to create spines.

The saguaro cactus with its curving arms is the type most people think of when they think of a cactus, and an easy one to create.

Crumple the foil into an armature to support the soft dough, preventing it from slumping into a glob. Add one or two arms to the base by wrapping another crumpled foil piece onto the base piece. Don't crush the foil too much, just enough to give it a cactus shape. It should be about 4" tall. To keep your cactus upright, flatten some foil to create a base.

Press a fist-sized piece of dough in place to cover the foil. Smooth the edges of dough pieces with your fingertips so it is smooth. Cover all the foil; don't let any show through. The dough will shrink a little as it dries, so be sure you have a thickness of at least 1/4" of dough over the foil.

Use a dinner fork to indent vertical lines in the dough to look like the ribs on a saguaro cactus.

Break the spaghetti into pieces about 3/4" long. Stick the pieces into the soft dough, so it looks as if the cactus is covered with spines.

Let dry for 24-36 hours.

A barrel cactus is simpler. Follow the same procedure as the saguaro, but use a foil armature shaped like a pear. Place small pear shapes at the base of the larger one, as they grow in clusters.

To create a nice effect, place the cacti on a small dish, and put some sand and pebbles around them. Use craft glue to stick on some colorful strawflower blossoms. Now you have a desert dish garden!

★ MATERIALS ★

Salt dough (Prepare one of the recipes that requires oven baking.)

Aluminum foil

Broom straws or toothpicks (whiskers)

6" length of yarn

Paint brush

$\frac{1}{4}$ cup of milk

Markers or paint for details

Crumple the aluminum foil into a ball, about the size of a golf ball. Roll or press the dough out flat, about $\frac{1}{2}$" thick. Cover the foil ball with the dough, smoothing the surface of the dough as you cover the foil. Shape the clay like a pear with a flat bottom, so the mouse will sit up.

Roll two tiny balls and flatten with your finger tip to create ears. Moisten and attach at the sides of the head. Roll a smaller ball for a nose; moisten and attach. Use a sharp pencil to poke eyes into the dough. Press the side of a straw's opening into the dough beneath the nose, to create a tiny smile. Stick some broomstraws or toothpicks about 2"-3" long into the dough to make whiskers.

Use a straight pin to prick tiny holes all over the surface to allow air to escape during baking. Prick about 1" apart, all over the mouse's body.

Using a paint brush, brush a thin coat of milk all over the mouse before baking.

Bake at 350° F for about 45 minutes. When cool, paint inside the ears and the nose. Use a fine-point marker to dot in the eyes. Seal with a clear coat of acrylic. Cut a 6" length of yarn for the tail. Use glue to attach the tail to the underside of the mouse body.

★ MATERIALS ★

Salt dough #2

Assorted glass jars with metal lids

Clear acrylic spray

Decorated dough-covered jar lids turn a plain pickle jar into a great gift idea. After the lids are baked, glue on candies, tiny decorations such as nutshell animals (see this chapter) or toys, or even dog biscuits, if the gift happens to be for your favorite pet.

The recipe for salt dough #2 makes enough to cover 6 to 9 jar lids.

Knead the dough until elastic. Divide into balls, one for each jar lid. Shape each ball over a jar lid.

Use a knife, spoon, fork or toothpick to make a design of holes and cuts on the dough. This is decorative, and also allows air to escape as the lid bakes.

Shapes can be formed from the remaining dough and stuck onto the covered lid. Moisten the dough slightly so the shapes stick better.

Place the dough-covered lids on a cookie sheet. Bake in the oven at 250° F for 2-3 hours or until hard and dry.

Cool.

Decorate the lids with paint or markers. Glue on candies or candy sprinkles. Spray with a clear acrylic coating.

Fill the jars with goodies and gently screw on the lids. Tie a festive ribbon around each jar, and give to a favorite person.

PRINTMAKING

Part of the fun of printmaking is getting to create several copies of your image. Prints make great greeting cards, gift wrap, decorations, or gifts themselves. When considering images to use for printmaking, pick one that is simple and clearly understood. Prints are most successful when there is little detail. Leave out all the little decorative lines. In the process of printing and repeating your design, details do not show up clearly and tend to make the print look fuzzy or messy.

Some printing projects require the use of brayers to pull the ink across a screen or other special equipment and inks. Those are interesting projects for older children or for times when an adult can help with setting up and cleaning up the work area. For other projects, washable inks are available. Acrylic paints or tempera paints can usually be substituted for colored inks.

Let's start with some simpler projects first.

Finger Painting

Finger paints

White paper

Use finger paints, painting either directly on a work tabletop or onto a cookie sheet. Using one color or several move the paint around with your fingers, until you have something you'd like to print. Lay a piece of white paper over the painted area, and rub the top of the paper lightly. Peel away gently and let dry.

Finger paint prints can be used as a background for drawing or painting, or you can print over a drawing done with colored chalk or crayon, giving it an unusual effect.

Thummies

Ink pad or tempera paint

Paper

Fine point felt-tip marking pen

Thummies are so easy to do, and you can continually come up with more ideas for them. Once you start, it's hard to stop!

If using an ink pad, simply press your thumb into the inked pad, and then press it onto paper. Add details and background to the print to create an animal, person or whatever strikes your fancy. If you are using tempera paint, pour a small amount into a jar lid or onto a styrofoam plate. You may need to gently wipe some off your fingertip before printing.

Thummies make great decorations for greeting cards, stationery and gift tags. They are a great way to illustrate a story or an experience. Thummies enjoy each other's company, and the more of them you put into a picture, the more fun it becomes.

If you get "artist's block" and can't think of a great idea to work on, look in the refrigerator! Fruits, vegetables and even fish offer tremendous printing possibilities.

Potatoes are easy to work with and don't cost very much. Cut a potato in half and use a toothpick to etch a design into the freshly cut area. Use a paring knife to cut away potato that you don't want in the design. Dip the cut edge of the potato into tempera paint, and press onto paper or cloth. Cutting simple shapes from the potato and then printing them in a pattern on the paper is very effective. Repeating the same shape but using a variety of colors is another possibility.

Other foods that are fun to use are:

Radishes. Cut lengthwise. Leave the greens on and dip them in green paint. Dip the radish in red paint, and press onto paper, cloth—even a tee shirt.

Lemons, limes, grapefruit. Cut crosswise.

Corn-on-the-cob. Roll in paint, then roll across the paper.

Mushrooms. Cut crosswise.

Cucumber. Cut in slices and cut designs into the peel.

Apples. Slice in half either lengthwise or crosswise. When you cut lengthwise, they print red heart shapes or red apple shapes onto paper. Cut crosswise, and they leave an unusual star pattern in the center.

Fish, kept frozen or chilled. Fish print best if ink is used, but tempera paints can be used as well. Lay the fish on newspaper or paper towels. Paint the surface with inks and gently lay a lightweight paper over the fish. Press lightly to imprint the fish onto the paper. Peel away and let dry. Use carrot or celery tops dipped in green paint to print plant shapes for your fish to hide in or swim behind.

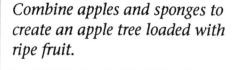
Sponge Printing

 MATERIALS

Sponges: Any kind will do. Look for cosmetic sponges, kitchen sponges, pieces of foam in a variety of shapes and textures.

Tempera paints

Dishes for paint

Paper

Pour paint into the dishes so it is easy to dip the sponges. Use scissors to cut the sponges into simple shapes: stars, hearts, trees, flowers, animals, letters of the alphabet, or whatever. Pieces of sponge or foam can be torn into unusual shapes, too.

Dip one side of the sponge into the paint, and press firmly onto your paper. Lift the sponge straight off the paper. Sponge printing is especially effective when you repeat the images several times. You can use it to create greeting cards, gift wrap paper, make pictures, picture frames or even to decorate tee shirts. Use like a stencil to decorate your bedroom walls! Use acrylic paints if you choose to paint on fabric or walls, so it is waterproof.

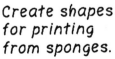
Create shapes for printing from sponges.

Combine apples and sponges to create an apple tree loaded with ripe fruit.

Apple Tree Print

 MATERIALS

18" x 24" white construction paper

Small apple. Cut in half lengthwise, leaving stem on one piece

Sponge pieces: Tear into 1" x 2" irregular pieces

Tempera paint: red, green, gold, brown

Paint brush

Dishes to hold paint

Use the brush and brown paint to paint a tree trunk with extended branches. Dip the sponge pieces into green and gold paint to daub leaf shapes onto the branches.

Dip the cut edge of the apple into the red paint, and print apples among the leaves and branches.

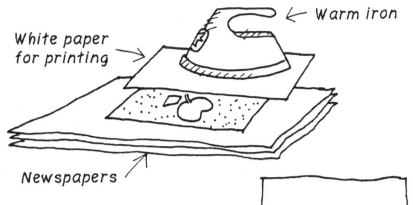

← Warm iron

White paper for printing

Newspapers

Color a design onto sandpaper.

The design will melt onto the white paper.

Block Prints

❤ MATERIALS ❤

Recycled egg carton

Construction paper

Pencil or ball point pen

Brayer

Water-based ink or tempera paint

Tray to pour ink on into

Newspapers

Sandpaper Prints

❤ MATERIALS ❤

Crayons

Sandpaper (sheets or used sander belts can be cut into smaller pieces)

White construction paper

Steam iron

Newspaper

With this type of printing, children can create colorful prints that resemble the vivid work of the impressionist artists. Don't try to achieve any detail in the finished picture.

Using bright, vibrant colored crayons, press firmly while coloring a design onto the sandpaper. Try to get as much crayon onto the sandpaper as possible. Lay down several layers of newspapers. Place the sandpaper piece on the newspapers, face up. Cover the sandpaper with the white paper. Iron on top of the paper lightly, at low heat, until the crayon just melts. Remove the paper. Let cool.

Use the flat lid of the egg carton. Cut off the edges so you have a flat rectangle. Draw a design on the surface by pressing into the lid with a blunt pencil or ball point pen, etching the pencil line into the lid. This technique is called intaglio.

Ink the surface of the lid with the brayer. Lay the paper over the inked piece, and rub the paper firmly so it picks up the inked design. Re-ink the design piece and print again; repeat as many times as you wish.

 MATERIALS ♥

Ball point ink pen
Large jar lid
Brayer
Brown printing ink or fabric paint
Piece of thick cardboard such as from boxes found in grocery stores
Craft glue
Red felt-tipped marking pen
White paper or fabric to print on (tee shirt, curtains, placemats, book cover, notepaper, gift wrap—you can print on almost anything)

Trace and cut bear from cardboard.
Use a pencil point to cut lines into the cardboard for details.

Glue bear to a jar lid to make printing easier.

Trace the teddy bear pattern onto paper and cut out. Trace around the cut-out onto the cardboard. Cut out the cardboard outline. Use a ball point pen to press into the cardboard, creating lines and details. Any area that is compressed by pushing down with the pen will not print, and will show up on the final project as a white line. Use the pen tip to etch in the features.

Glue the cardboard bear shape to the jar lid. The jar lid holds it firm, and keeps your fingers out of the ink when printing.

Use the brayer to apply ink or paint to the surface of the bear shape. Press down firmly to print on paper or cloth. When paint is dry, use the marking pen to color in the bow tie.

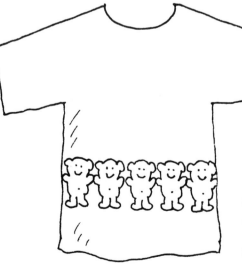

Print on shirts, bags, notebooks.

Use acrylic paints for these projects.

♥ MATERIALS ♥

Cardboard

Glue

Newspapers

Ink or tempera paint

Brayer

Paper or cloth to print on

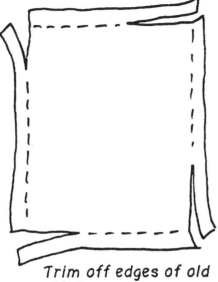

Trim off edges of old gift box.

Cut out a design from another piece of cardboard.

Glue the cut-out design onto the other piece of cardboard.

Use discarded cardboard, tagboard or gift boxes. First cut a backing piece of cardboard the size of the picture you want to print. Start with a small piece, about 8" x 10". Trace and cut out a design from another piece of cardboard. Glue it to the cardboard backing. This will be the printing block.

Cover your work area with plenty of newspapers. You can use ink or tempera paints to print images on paper or cloth. Lay your cardboard printing block on the newspapers, with the design side facing up. Apply ink or paint with a brayer.

Lay a piece of paper or cloth over the inked block, and press gently over the entire surface, so the ink will stick. Peel away and let dry.

Practice by printing on pieces of newsprint the first few times. Begin with designs that use only one color of ink. After some experience, you can brush on particular colors in certain areas of your design, to create a multicolor print.

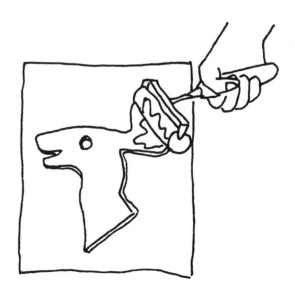

Apply ink or paint with a brayer.

❤ MATERIALS ❤

Top of box or old frame
Nylon fabric
Masking tape
Newsprint
Fingerpaint
Scissors
Cardboard squeegee
Stapler
Construction paper

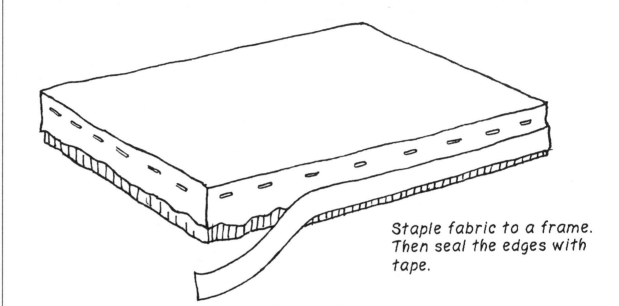

Staple fabric to a frame. Then seal the edges with tape.

Silk screen printing is actually a stencil method of printing. Paint is forced through a piece of stretched mesh fabric that has been prepared with a design, and the paint is printed onto fabric or paper.

Silk screen is a good way to create several prints of the same image. Greeting cards, gift tags, and posters can be easily made this way.

First you need to prepare a screen. You can use silk, nylon or other mesh material. Special silk screen fabric is available in art supply stores. You can also use nylon stockings or sheer curtain material. A screen is made from a box top with the center cut out, or an old picture frame.

Stretch the mesh fabric tight and attach it to the box by stapling. It is important to keep it very tight. Seal all around the edge of the fabric with masking tape. There must be no spaces or holes.

For young children, a simple silk screen can be made by using an embroidery hoop. Just clamp in the nylon and you're ready to go.

Next make the stencil for printing. Trace the size of your screen and cut the stencil paper the same size. Use newsprint for making the stencil. Fold the stencil paper in half and cut a design from the center fold.

The stencil is used under the screen. Be sure it blocks all areas

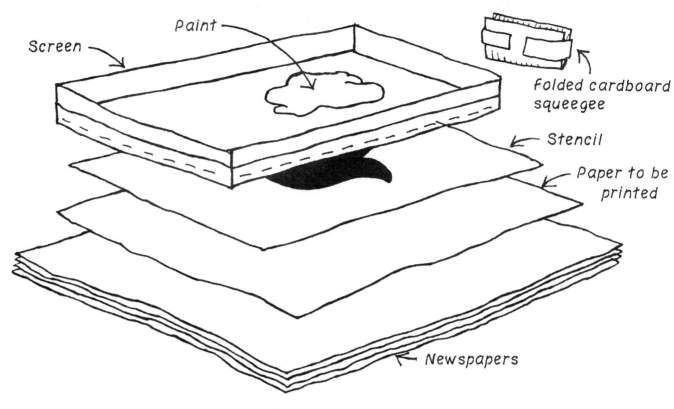

Screen

Paint

folded cardboard squeegee

Stencil

Paper to be printed

Newspapers

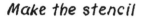

Make the stencil

that are not to be printed. Remember that paint will be forced through any openings in the stencil. Make a squeegee with a piece of cardboard by folding it in half and taping it together. Use it for pushing the paint through the screen.

Ready to print! Place the paper to be printed on your table (covered with lots of newspapers). Put the stencil on top of the paper. Lay the screen on top of the stencil.

Drop a teaspoon of fingerpaint on top of the screen at one end. Using the squeegee, pull the paint from one end of the screen to the other, letting it go through the open areas of the stencil. The paint will cause the stencil to adhere to the screen and will print at the same time. The first print may not be exactly as you want it, so practice on newsprint at first.

When you're pleased with your practice prints, try printing

on a piece of colored construction paper. One of the best things about silk screening is that you can make many prints of your image.

Carved Rubber Stamps

❤ MATERIALS ❤

Erasers
Pen
Craft knife
Straight pins

Rubber stamps are so much fun, and everyone can use them. They can be made from a wide variety of odds and ends found at home.

Rubber stamps can be made from erasers; the large pink kind are the best. Use an ink pen to draw the outline you wish to print. Then, use a craft knife to cut away eraser surface outside the lines. You can use a straight pin to dig out tiny detail areas.

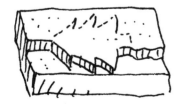

Draw a design on the eraser. Cut away eraser outside of the design.

Here'sanothertechnique to create many stamps for little money. Use shoe insoles, the kind sold in the drug store that can be cut to size. They are made from a thin layer of foam with a layer of latex on one side.

Some insoles have fabric backing on one side, but use the smoother latex side for inking. It is also easy to draw your design on the latex side, using a ball point pen.

Draw your chosen outline, and cut out carefully with scissors. You can glue the cut-out to a small wooden scrap or block which will make printing easy and keep your hands clean. If you don't have wooden blocks, use old metal jar lids. Glue the insole cut-out to the block or jar lid with rubber cement.

When the cement dries, you are ready to print. Use a regular inked stamp pad.

Some ideas for stamp designs are: trees, hearts, boats, flowers, butterflies, simple letters or short names or greetings. You might want to try small fish, bunnies, shamrocks, Easter eggs, or faces.

Rubber Sole Stamps

❤ MATERIALS ❤

Shoe insoles
Ball point pen
Scissors
Rubber cement
Wooden block or jar lid

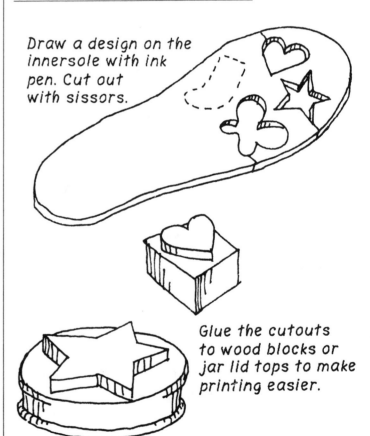

Draw a design on the innersole with ink pen. Cut out with sissors.

Glue the cutouts to wood blocks or jar lid tops to make printing easier.

SCULPTURE

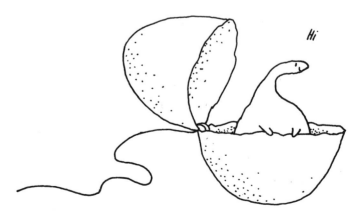
Hi

PLASTER PROJECTS

Plaster is an inexpensive and easy medium to work with. It is exciting to use, and it hardens. This is super for crafts, but a problem for sinks and drains. When using plaster, have plenty of newspaper to cover work surfaces and two buckets—one to mix the plaster in and one filled with water for rinsing off spoons and hands. I also keep a roll of paper towels handy. Plaster is not a problem, if you don't pour it down the sink or even wash anything off in your sink. Use the bucket and when you're finished, toss the water in the bucket into the shrubbery or on the driveway. Just don't wash any of it down the drain.

Plaster of Paris is inexpensive. It can be purchased in craft stores in small amounts or in building supply centers by the hundred-pound sack. It is cheaper to buy it in the large sack, if you have use for the larger quantity.

Keep dry plaster in a covered container. A coffee can or small garbage can is fine. Plaster absorbs moisture and hardens, if not kept dry. I like to save milk jugs for mixing up small batches. Cut the top quarter of the jug away with scissors. Then you can toss the jug out when you are finished, saving on clean-up.

Projects are wet when finished, so set out plenty of newspapers to dry them on.

Mixing plaster: There is no need to measure or weigh portions. Use approximately two parts of plaster to one part of water. I do it the easy way. Fill the container half full with water (using warm water speeds setting time). Then, using a cup, I sprinkle the surface of the water with plaster. Continue adding plaster by gently sprinkling on the surface. When the plaster stops sinking out of sight into the water, you have added enough. It will start to "island" and float on the surface of the water. At this point, it is a saturated solution and no more plaster is necessary. Stir gently and slowly. Try to keep air bubbles from forming in the plaster. Let the mixture stand until it starts to thicken; then pour into the molding container you have prepared earlier.

Plaster usually sets up in about 15-20 minutes. Using warm water or a little salt will speed that up. To slow the setting time, add a small amount of vinegar, alcohol or sugar to the mixture.

Wall Plaques

★ MATERIALS ★

Coffee can lid

Plaster of Paris

Toothpicks or pencil

Decorative materials

Paper clip

Wall plaques are all-time plaster favorites. They are easy to do and always look good, expressing the artist's mood at the moment. Use a coffee can lid for a base. Pour the thickened plaster into the lid. Press a handprint—or a pet's pawprint—into the almost hard plaster. You can also drop assorted materials into the plaster to create a design or design anything that suits your fancy. Use a toothpick to inscribe a name and date on the plaque.

Before the plaster hardens, insert a large paper clip, or a soda can pop-top into the top edge of the plaque, so it can be hung on the wall later.

Pour plaster into plastic lid.

Print something in it. Stick a paper clip or pop-top ring in it. When hard, pop the plaster away from the lid.

Relief Sculpture

★ MATERIALS ★

Aluminum pie tin

One pound of modeling clay (like Plastilina)

Plaster of Paris

Paper clip

Press modeling clay into a pie tin, one-half inch thick. Use fingertips and tools to inscribe a scene or design. Stick on pieces of clay, or cut into some parts to give the scene three dimensions.

Mix plaster. When it starts to thicken, pour into the pie pan, covering the clay completely. The plaster should be 1" thick. Insert a clip for hanging. Let the plaster dry and set twenty-four hours before removing. Gently lift the plaster up from the clay. Use a table knife to gently separate the two. Rub away any tiny bits of clay that cling to the plaster. When the plaque is dry (it will no longer feel cold to the touch), sand rough edges and stain with some paint or rub in shoe polish and buff to a soft shine.

MOLDING WITH PLASTER

Save any plastic bubble-wrap packages that you find. They come on make-up packages and are used for any small items sold on a cardboard backing. (It would be much better for our environment if we didn't use plastics. If you do find these items, please make every effort to recycle them through many projects.) They make interesting molds for plaster. Sometimes you can find one in a shape that suggests an animal; other times,

you may need to stretch your imagination. Rub a little oil or petroleum jelly onto the mold to prevent the plaster from sticking, and fill the plastic mold to the top with plaster. Insert a bent paper clip into the wet plaster, if you want to hang your creation on a wall or Christmas tree. When completely dry, pop the plaster out and save the plastic bubble for another project. Paint an abstract design on your plaster decoration.

It's fun to work with plaster outdoors. Look for soft mud with a variety of animal tracks. Mix and pour your plaster into the tracks. When hardened, lift the plaster piece gently from the mud. At the beach, dig out a small hole in the soft sand. Lay a few sea shells or rocks with barnacles on the bottom and sides of the hole. Pour your mixed plaster into the hole. Remove it when it has set. If you don't like the clinging sand, brush it off gently, but it does give it an interesting texture.

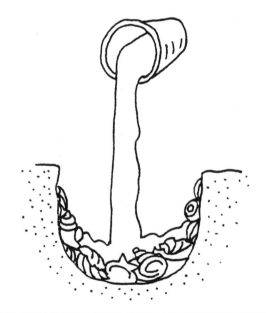

PAPIER-MACHE

Papier-mache is one of the most exciting and least expensive sculpting media to use. It can be used to make simple items like bowls or more intricate work, such as jewelry or puppets. You can purchase premixed papier-mache compounds at craft shops. These mix up instantly when water is added. Or, you can create your own from flour, water and old newspapers or paper grocery bags.

While papier-mache is fun to use, it also quite possibly makes the biggest mess of any medium. It can be cleaned up easily with paper towels and water, while it is still wet; after it dries, however, it becomes quite stubborn and difficult to clean up. Cover all work areas and project drying areas with layers of newspapers. Working with papier-mache is the perfect project to do outdoors, and a sunny day helps the projects dry more quickly.

To get started with any papier-mache project, gather up newspapers and tear into strips, about 1" x 3" for most projects. Gather up containers for mixing the gluing mixture and some paper towels for messy hands.

The paper strips are layered and glued to make a strong, laminated surface which dries hard and can then be sanded and painted. If you want to create large animals or sculptures, use a base or frame under the papier-mache.

A base can be almost anything that supports the paper strips until they are dry. Large shapes can be created by using pieces of wood or dowels and chicken wire. Smaller objects can be formed around wadded paper balls, rolled and tied newspapers, crumpled aluminum foil, cardboard boxes, or inflated balloons. Papier-mache can also be pressed into a mold which has been greased with petroleum jelly. When the paper strips are dry, pull the sculpture away from the mold.

To make the glue mixture, you can use wallpaper paste, or a flour and water mixture. If you choose to use the wallpaper paste, either the premixed variety or the powdered kind works fine. Add water until it's the consistency of creamy gravy. The homemade flour-water paste is con-venient to use because it is handy and inexpensive. Just mix it with water in a bowl, and begin dipping the paper strips. If you choose to do your project somewhere else, like outdoors or with a group, save a milk jug. Mix your flour and water glue, and pour into the jug. Cap it and it will travel well. Then just pour out what you need into an aluminum pie plate. The glue mixture keeps for a few days, covered in the refrigerator. After a short time it begins to smell, so I usually make up only what I need for one session.

Papier-mache projects need several days' drying time between application of layers of strips. The damp projects must be set in an area with good air circulation or they may begin to mold and smell. A warm open area is fine.

Decorating a papier-mache project is the most fun! You can use any kind of paint and can also glue on sequins, beads, trimmings, anything you wish. When your painted project is dry, give it a spray of clear acrylic so it will shine. Papier-mache looks great when finished with bright, shiny acrylic paints. You can also give the finished project a coat or two of flat white latex paint to seal and strengthen, before finishing with watercolors, marking pens or tempera paints.

PAPIER-MACHE BOWL

MATERIALS

Flour and water for glue mixture; use a ratio of one cup flour to one cup water.

Newspaper or grocery bag strips, 1" x 3"

Petroleum jelly (Vaseline)

Bowl

Tempera paint

Acrylic gloss finish

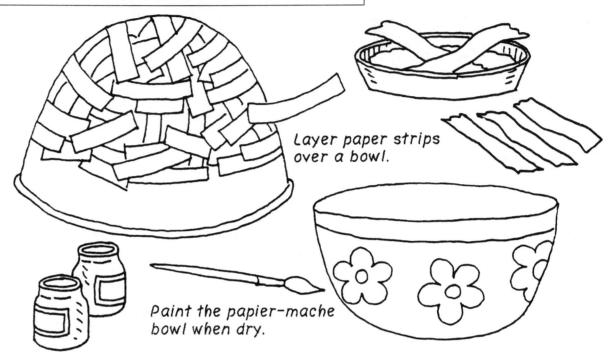

Layer paper strips over a bowl.

Paint the papier-mache bowl when dry.

You can create really bright Indian-type bowls using papier-mache. The bowl is made by layering paper strips over a mold (a bowl).

Cover the outside, bottom and rim of the bowl with petroleum jelly. This makes it easier to separate the dried bowl from the mold when you have completed your project.

Cover the outside of the bowl with strips of newspaper dipped in the glue mixture. Apply the strips vertically, covering the bowl's surface. Then apply a second layer of strips horizontally. Apply a third layer, vertically again. Repeat this layering, until the papier-mache is five layers thick.

Let dry. Separate the papier-mache bowl from the bowl used as a mold. You may have to insert the tip of a table knife at the edges and pry apart to loosen the bowls. Paint the bowl with tempera and when the paint dries, give it two coats of an acrylic sealer.

Your papier-mache bowl will look wonderful holding items like potpourri, potato chips, or anything else you want. It can be gently wiped clean, but don't try to wash it in water.

★ **MATERIALS** ★

Balloon*

Paper strips, 1" x 3"

Glue mixture (flour and water)

Tempera paints

Tissue paper:
bright blue, green and brown

Drinking glass or mug

Paper clip

Fishing line

There are many things to make using a balloon as a mold for papier-mache. A model of our planet looks really nice hanging from a piece of fishing line from a ceiling. Because your balloon probably won't create a perfectly shaped sphere, it is going to be even more scientifically accurate because our planet isn't a perfectly shaped sphere, either.

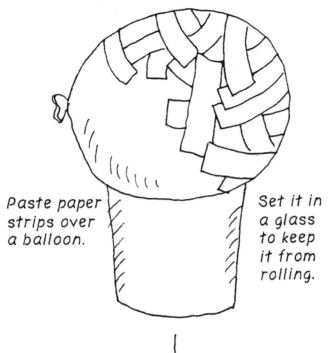

Paste paper strips over a balloon.

Set it in a glass to keep it from rolling.

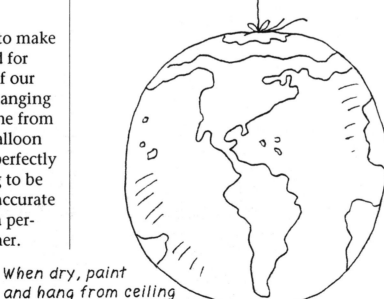

When dry, paint and hang from ceiling with fishing line.

Blow up the balloon and tie the end closed. Cover the balloon surface with three or four layers of paper strips dipped in the glue mixture. Insert the clip for hanging. Use the drinking glass or mug to support the balloon while you work, so it won't roll around on the table. Allow it to dry.

Paint in the continents and oceans with appropriate colors or use small torn pieces of colored tissue paper. Dip the tissue papers in the glue mixture and then layer them in the appropriate places. Use the brown and green colors for continents, and the blue for oceans. You can wad small balls and glue in place for mountain ranges or islands. Then cover with a layer of more tissue pieces. When dry, coat with an acrylic spray and hang with fishing line.

Warning: Young children can swallow deflated balloons. Please supervise carefully.

DINOSAURS

Papier-Mache Pulp

It's easy to make a thick pulp that can be molded into shapes like clay, or pressed into molds, dried and painted.

Tear newspaper or pulp paper egg cartons into small pieces and soak in warm water for several hours. Squeeze the excess water out. Sprinkle dry wall-paper paste over the pulp and knead with your hands. Work with your fingers, until the pulp becomes smooth and pliable.

The pulp mache can be used to create unique puppet or doll heads, small animal shapes, or anything that can be shaped by hand. It can also be pressed into candy molds, or gelatin molds that have been covered with petroleum jelly. Papier-mache pulp has been used for a long time, and was popular in the Victorian era when used to create carved-looking picture frames, vases, and small tables.

*See warning, page 69.

MATERIALS

Balloons*
Torn paper strips, 1" x 3"
Glue mixture (flour and water, consistency of thick gravy)
Lightweight cardboard (milk cartons and cereal boxes are good sources)
Paper tubes (from toilet tissue or paper wrap)
Small boxes, like gelatin boxes
Newspapers
Masking tape
Paints: tempera, acrylic or latex

Three types of dinosaurs are easy to make using the paper strip technique. All use a balloon for the tummy area, small boxes for the head, and small paper tubes for legs.

Following the drawings, place several layers of paper strips over the blown-up balloon; then tape on the neck

TYRANNOSAURUS REX

Head is a gelatin box—cut it on 3 sides and fold in half.

Arms are made from rolled paper.

Tape a cardboard strip to his back.

Rolled and taped paper for tail.

Legs are paper tubes.

feet are cut from cardboard.

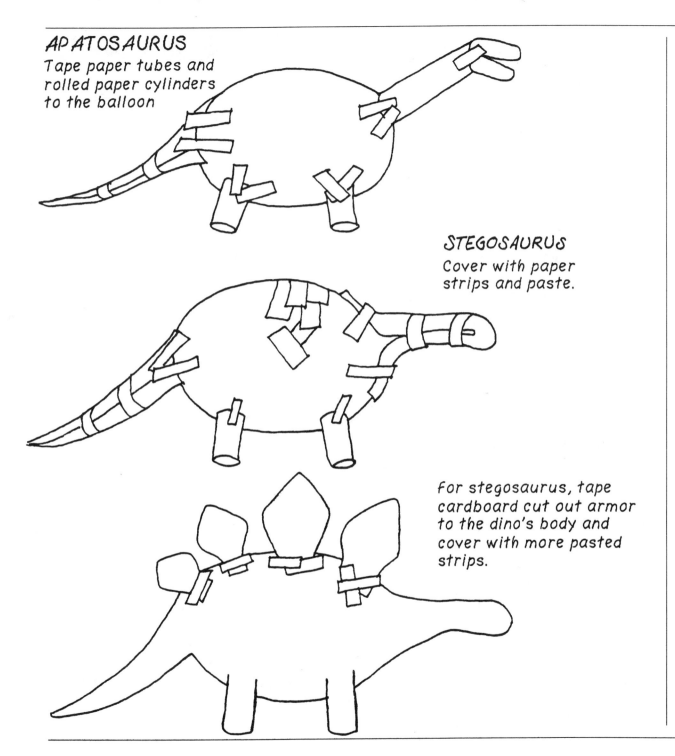

APATOSAURUS
Tape paper tubes and rolled paper cylinders to the balloon

STEGOSAURUS
Cover with paper strips and paste.

For stegosaurus, tape cardboard cut out armor to the dino's body and cover with more pasted strips.

and head section. When dry, tape on the paper tubes for the legs and tail sections. When they dry, add spines cut from lightweight cardboard. Feet and hands are cut from the cardboard and taped in place. Layer paperstrips over the feet and spines, until the whole creature is several layers thick. Allow to dry. Glue on odds and ends to create texture and detail. Use buttons for eyes or glue on paper reinforcements for eyes. Teeth can be made by gluing on rice or inserting broken toothpicks into the damp mouth area before the paper strips are dry. Lentils glued over the entire surface of the creature's body create a reptilian skin texture.

Paint the finished dinosaur and add final details. You can glue on toenails cut from lightweight cardboard. I like to trim off part of a red or pink balloon, and glue it inside the mouth so it looks like a rubbery tongue.

Give your finished creature a spray coating of clear acrylic gloss to protect it and help preserve it.

★ MATERIALS ★

Balloon*
Newspaper strips, 1" x 3"
Glue mixture
Small toy dinosaur or one made from clay
String, about 30" long
Tape

This egg will really hatch! Surprise your friends when the baby dinosaur hidden in the egg pops out.

Blow up the balloon and tie the end securely. Tape one end of the string to the center of the balloon's middle. Wrap it around the balloon once, and let the loose end of the string hang loose. Being careful not to get the loose string covered with strips, cover the entire balloon (including the one wrap of string) with a layer of damp strips. Wrap the hanging string around the balloon again, and let the loose end hang free.

Tape string to the balloon and wrap it around one time.

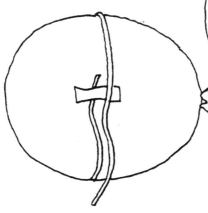

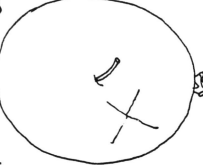

Paste paper strips over the string letting the loose end hang free.

When strips are dry, cut an "X" in the egg and insert a dinosaur.

Cover with another layer of strips. Continue until the string is almost used up and the balloon is covered with several layers of string and papier-mache strips. Leave about 1" of string exposed.

Allow the egg to dry. Using a razor blade or sharp knife, cut two slits in the shape of an "x" in the side of the egg. The balloon inside will pop. Insert the tiny dinosaur into the egg, and cover the opening with two or three damp strips. Dry. Then paint the egg with tempera paint.

See warning, page 69.

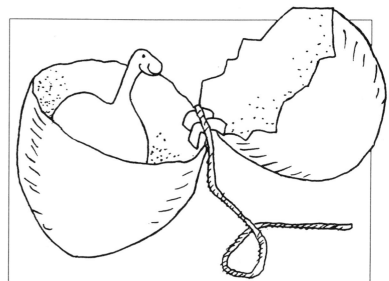

To hatch the dinosaur egg and release the tiny dinosaur, pull on the tiny piece of string that is left on the surface of the egg. Pull gently on the string and the egg will pop apart into two halves.

★ MATERIALS ★

Paper tubes (use paper towel rolls, tissue rolls, or for giant bones, use tubes from gift wrap)

Newspaper or grocery bag strips, 1" x 4"

Masking tape

Glue mixture (flour and water, consistency of thick gravy)

Tempera paint or latex house paint

Newspapers

These bones will remind you of the Flintstones! You can make them any size, depending upon the size of your paper tube. If you don't have a large enough tube, make one by taping a large piece of tagboard or lightweight cardboard into a cylinder.

Tape crumpled paper balls to both ends of the tube. Cover with pasted strips of paper.

Crush several sheets of newspaper into balls, wrapping crushed sheets with more sheets until they are the size you want. Use masking tape to secure the balls to the ends of the tubes.

Using the torn strips and glue mixture, place three or four layers of strips over the entire bone. Shape the ends while damp, adding more strips as desired to give the ends a bone shape.

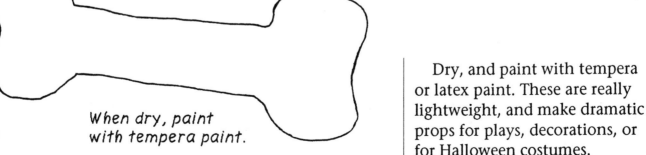

When dry, paint with tempera paint.

Dry, and paint with tempera or latex paint. These are really lightweight, and make dramatic props for plays, decorations, or for Halloween costumes.

STUFFED PAPER SCULPTURE

Newsapers
(for stuffing the sculpture)

Butcher paper, newsprint
or newspapers

Stapler and staples

Paints: tempera or acrylics

Paper sculptures are lots of fun because they are big, colorful and unique. Before you begin, decide what you would like to enlarge or exaggerate. Large paper fish are easy to create. But think of what would be unusual. How about a large, stuffed insect? Camera? Ear of corn? With stuffed paper sculpture, there is no limit to what you can create.

Draw the desired shape on the paper and cut out two identical shapes, one for a front, one for the back. Staple the two pieces together until about half the object is stapled. Then begin wadding up newspapers and stuffing the sculpture. Staple the edges as the stuffing fills it up, until the entire shape is full, and stapled shut. Lay the sculpture on a table top covered with newspapers, and begin painting the surface. If you like, use yarn, strips of paper, crepe paper streamers, or whatever you choose, to add to your sculpture.

When dry, you can perch your creation on a shelf, or tie on fishing line at the top, and hang from your ceiling. These three-dimensional paper sculptures can also be displayed by drilling a hole in a flat piece of wood and inserting a dowel or broomstick. Insert the other end of the dowel into the bottom of the sculpture.

Staple front to back along edges.
Leave an opening for stuffing.
Stuff with crumpled newspapers.

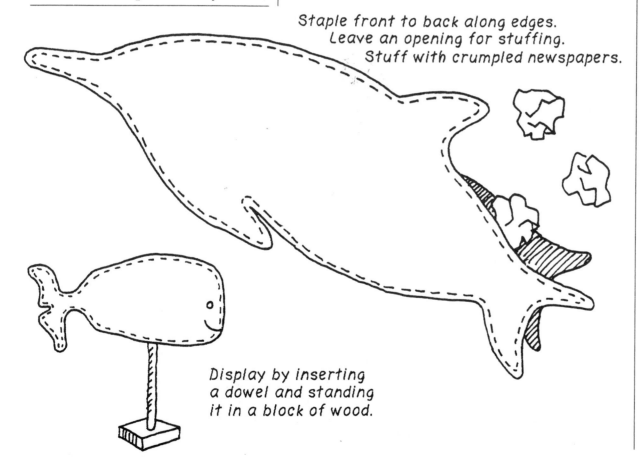

Display by inserting
a dowel and standing
it in a block of wood.

CRUSHED FOIL SCULPTURE

★ **MATERIALS** ★

Aluminum foil

Newspapers

Cardboard square about 12" x12"

There are several ways to model with aluminum foil. One way is to model a sculpture out of crushed newspaper shapes and then cover it with aluminum foil. Another way is to use the crushed aluminum foil as a base (or armature) which is then covered with papier-mache. Or, you can use aluminum foil alone to create interesting abstract or realistic shapes.

When beginning work with foil, use a piece about 9"x 12" to experiment. Work with the foil a bit, crushing, crumpling, pulling apart, and modeling like clay. Tear off small pieces and press back into the surface. Use a pencil point to push in texture and detail.

With foil, you can create recognizable forms, such as people, animals or objects, but, you can't create a lot of fine detail. Try to create the general outline or outer contour of the object rather than small areas of detail.

Start with the basic shapes of everyday articles like fruits, vegetables, chairs and cars. Then, try to make some people in action.

When you have completed your sculpture, cover the cardboard base with aluminum foil, and glue the sculpture to the base for display. Use a hot glue gun for quick and secure attachment.

Crush foil into shapes and press them together.

Smooth the surface and cover with more foil.

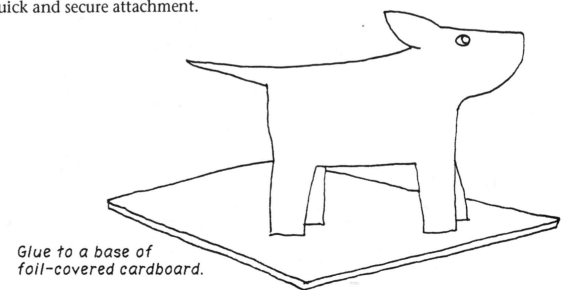

Glue to a base of foil-covered cardboard.

Coil and wrap wire
to create an object.
Glue to a base.

★ **MATERIALS** ★

Lightweight wire: coat hangers, telephone wire, stovepipe wire, fine gauge picture hanging wire.

Display bases made from: clay, wood, cork, cardboard.

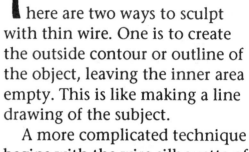

Create an
outline of
the object.

Glue to a wood base.

There are two ways to sculpt with thin wire. One is to create the outside contour or outline of the object, leaving the inner area empty. This is like making a line drawing of the subject.

A more complicated technique begins with the wire silhouette of the object which is then covered with thin wire. Wind the wire in spirals, wrapping it around the form until it is three-dimensional and can stand alone. Then, tuck the wire ends inside the body of the sculpture.

After attaching the sculpture to the base with staples or a hot glue gun, the whole thing can be painted with spray enamel. Finished wire sculptures look very dynamic and sophisticated. They make nice gifts to put on a desk or bookcase.

TOOTHPICK SCULPTURE

 ★ MATERIALS ★

★ **MATERIALS** ★

Toothpicks (flat ones are easier to work with)

Two paper plates

White glue

Enamel spray paint

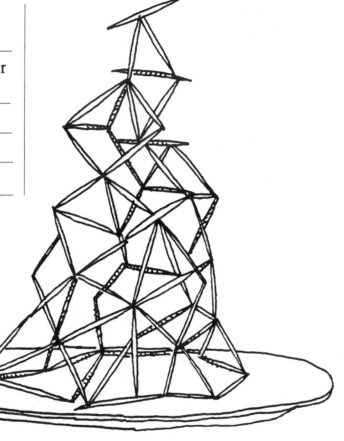

Dip toothpick ends in glue and position them in an interesting arrangement.

This type of sculpture results in free-form, very modern looking constructions. Any age group will enjoy this project. It is inexpensive and keeps most young sculptors engrossed quite a while. The gluing is done piece by piece. Allow plenty of time to complete the structure.

Squirt white glue out onto a paper plate. Use the other paper plate as the sculpture's base. Dip the toothpick ends into the glue, and arrange them on the plate, building the sculpture upwards. As the glue sets, add more toothpicks, building up in height and width to create a three-dimensional structure. When the glue is dry, spray the entire piece with glossy enamel spray paint; spray the plate as well. This gives the sculpture strength, as well as a finished look.

For a variation, you may want to use drinking straws, cotton swabs (like Q-tips), or coffee stirrer sticks instead of the toothpicks.

Young children can make fabric soft sculpture, if an adult is available to help them operate the sewing machine or do the sewing for them. Older children can practice a basic running stitch to sew their own sculptures together.

Any design can be turned into soft sculpture: foods, objects, animals. You can enlarge items to giant size: like a huge stuffed button or bagel. You can also create wonderful dolls and teddy bears this way.

Fold a piece of fabric in half. Sketch an outline and rough details with pencil on it. Use the markers to outline the shape. Add a 1/4" border around the entire shape. This is the seam allowance. Cut out the shape, cutting through both layers of fabric at once. This gives a front and back that are identical and can be sewn together.

Pin the back and front pieces together, with the right sides facing each other. Sew around the figure, stitching about 1/4" from the edge of the fabric. Leave an opening of 3" or 4" for turning and stuffing. Clip the seam allowances at the curved areas, so they lie smooth after turning and

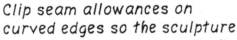

★ MATERIALS ★

Unbleached muslin or bed sheets or fabric scraps
Felt tip markers
Scissors
Stuffing materials: polyfill, old nylons, fabric scraps
Sewing supplies
Sewing machine (optional)

Clip seam allowances on curved edges so the sculpture will lie flat when turned right side out.

Leave an opening for turning and stuffing.

stuffing. Turn the object right side out, and begin stuffing.

Roll the cut edges of fabric to the inside and pin. Using a needle and thread take small stitches to close the opening. You can also sew the opening shut with a sewing machine.

Finish the sculpture by coloring with markers or paints if you choose. Bits of yarn, fur, feathers, sequins or whatever can be glued on to decorate.

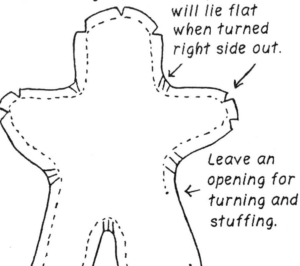

Yarn makes good hair. Glue it on, or sew to the head with a large needle.

Turn, Stuff, sew opening closed. Decorate and make clothes for your doll.

SPRING IS HERE

 MATERIALS

Empty cardboard ice cream container, with top and bottom cut out

Colored construction paper

White glue

String

Crepe paper or tissue paper

Paper punch

Scissors

Cover the empty container by gluing various colors of construction paper over it. Cut long streamers from the crepe paper or tissue paper, and glue them to one open end of the container. Cut out shapes from paper scraps and glue to the outside of the container for decoration.

Punch four holes in the other end of the container, spacing them equally around the rim. Thread string through the holes and double knot. Tie all four strands together at the top. Tie one longer piece of string to the knotted ends and use it to hang your windsock from the edge of a deck, roof or tree branch.

ROBIN'S NEST WITH EGGS

 MATERIALS

Salt dough #4 recipe
(see page 45): some colored
yellow-brown,
and some colored light blue.

Garlic press

Squeeze the yellow-brown dough through the garlic press to create "straw" to build the bird's nest. Shape the straw pieces into a rounded nest.

Roll small lumps of blue dough into egg-shaped balls. Moisten the bottom of each "egg" and stick it into the nest. Let air-dry until hard.

Eggs are blue
salt dough.

Tan salt dough

Baby Chick

❀ MATERIALS ❀

Cotton balls

Yellow powder tempera paint

Baby powder

Paper sack

Orange and black construction paper

Paper hole punch

White glue

Half of an eggshell, washed and dried

You can buy yellow puffs at craft shops, or you can make your own using baby powder and cotton balls. Place a couple of spoonfuls of the yellow powder tempera and a little baby powder into a paper sack. Add two cotton balls to the sack and fold the top closed. Shake the balls in the powder. Remove the cotton balls and shake lightly over the open sack.

Glue one colored cotton ball in the half eggshell and the other ball on top of the first one.

Punch out two black eyes and cut out an orange beak from the colored paper. Glue in place.

Glue 2 yellow puffs to make a chick. Glue in an eggshell half.
Glue eyes and mouth in place. Glue eggshell to a card so it will stand up.

fold
Mouth: use orange paper.

Eyes: cut or punch from black paper.

Spring Bunnies

❀ MATERIALS ❀

Construction paper, white and pink

Cotton balls

Paste or tape

For each bunny, cut an 8¹/₂" x 11" piece of pink construction paper into two pieces, one 5" x 11" and the other 3¹/₂" x 11". Cut out two ears from one end of the smaller strip of paper. Cut out two white circles for eyes.

Roll the pieces into two loops. Paste or tape to hold the position. The ears should be in the middle of the two loops. Glue the two eyes on the smaller loop, and a cotton ball on the back of the large loop for a tail.

Eggshell Mosaic

 MATERIALS

White eggshells, rinsed and dried

Food coloring

Vinegar

Hot water

White glue

Cotton swabs (like Q-tips)

Construction paper

Save eggshells until you have enough for a project. Rinse and let them dry. Crush and store them in a container. When you have a couple dozen eggs' worth, make up some dye by filling a jar with ½ cup of hot water. Add a teaspoon of vinegar and a few drops of food coloring. Drop some of the crushed shells into the water.

Let them soak a few minutes. Spoon them out and allow to dry on a cookie sheet. (Hurry this up by drying on the cookie sheet in a 200° F oven.)

When you have a good assortment of different colored shells, get your construction paper and glue. Using the cotton swab, paint a design on the paper using the glue. Then, sprinkle the colored eggshells onto the glue, and shake off the excess.

For variety, you can also use plain white eggshells on colored paper.

Apply the paint and let it run together.

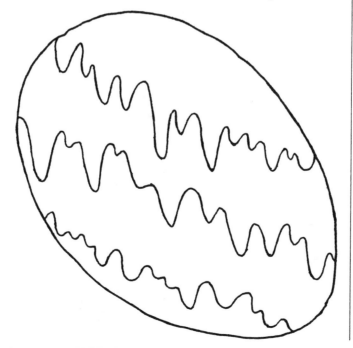

Glossy Eggs

 MATERIALS

Sweetened condensed milk (one can)

Food coloring

White construction paper

Paint brushes or cotton swabs

Cut large white egg shapes out of white construction paper. Mix four different colors of food coloring with the condensed milk in four separate paint cups. Keep the colors bright and pastel.

Use brushes or cotton swabs to generously paint the eggs in different colors as shown. While the paint is still wet, hang the eggs on a bulletin board with push pins, slanting the egg at an angle. Allow the egg paintings to dry. The paint colors will run together, creating designs that run in a diagonal direction. Allow them to dry for several days, until the paint is dry and shines like enamel.

PAPIER-MACHE EASTER EGGS

❀ **MATERIALS** ❀

Balloon*

Newspaper strips

Glue mixture

Tempera paints

See the papier-mache section (page 67) for details on how to use paper strips and a glue mixture. When you have your strips and glue mixture prepared, blow up a rounded balloon and knot the end. Cover the balloon with paper strips and glue. Build up three or more smooth layers of paper. Be sure to cover the knotted end of the balloon. Let dry. Use tempera paints mixed in pastel colors to paint the papier-mache, decorating in an Easter or spring theme. Or look in a field guide and paint the eggs to look like different bird eggs. When the paint is dry, you can spray the egg with clear acrylic finish, if desired.

Make a huge basket to hold your giant eggs.

Use brown and green butcher paper. Take about four feet of brown butcher paper, fold it in half lengthwise, twice, and staple the ends together to create a large circle. This will be the basket. Use another length of brown paper, folded and stapled, to create a handle for the basket. Staple the ends to the sides of the basket. To fill your basket with grass, cut green paper (butcher paper, crepe paper, or tissue) into 1"-wide strips, and fill the basket with them. Then add your giant papier-mache eggs to create a real eye-popping display.

See warning, page 69.

6" square piece of paper

Pencil with eraser

Straight pin

Scissors

If using white paper, color or paint a colorful, abstract design. Place design face down. Draw dots on the corners and center of the paper. Cut along the dotted lines as shown, but don't cut all the way through the center of the square.

Fold the corners into the center of the square, lining up the dots on top of each other.

Push the straight pin through the corner dots, through the dot in the center of the square, and into the side of the pencil's eraser. Blow into the pinwheel, and watch it spin!

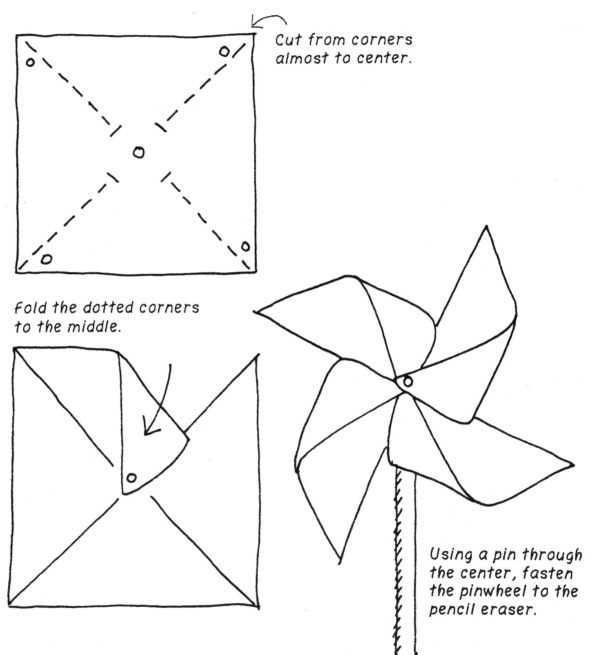

Cut from corners almost to center.

Fold the dotted corners to the middle.

Using a pin through the center, fasten the pinwheel to the pencil eraser.

 MATERIALS

Construction or typing paper: colored or white

Tissue paper: a tiny piece of yellow, and a piece of green about 12" x 24"

Drinking straw

Pencil

Scissors

Glue

Tape or stapler

*T*race the petal pattern onto the typing paper. Cut it out. Fold along the dotted lines to create the flower. Glue the last petal to the first one as shown. Leave the bottom open a bit to allow space for the stem to stick through.

Cut a 1" x 1" piece of yellow tissue paper. Glue it to cover one end of the straw.

Cut leaf shapes from the green tissue. Cut two strips of green tissue paper, about 1" x 24". Wrap these green strips around the straw, covering it completely. Glue the two ends securely.

Insert the covered straw into the base of the flower. Tape or staple in place. Wrap another strip of green tissue to cover the stapled area.

Glue or tape the leaves to the stem.

To give your flower the final touch that makes it really look like a lily, roll the petals around a pencil to give them a curled, natural look. Now, make a whole bouquet to fill a vase with springtime.

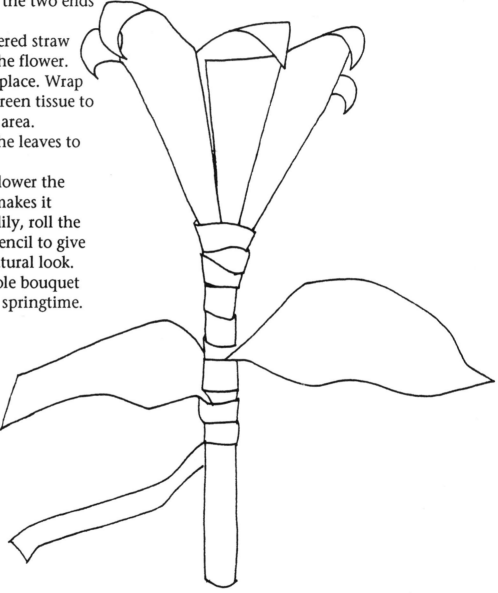

THIS IS *A FULL SIZE PATTERN PIECE!*

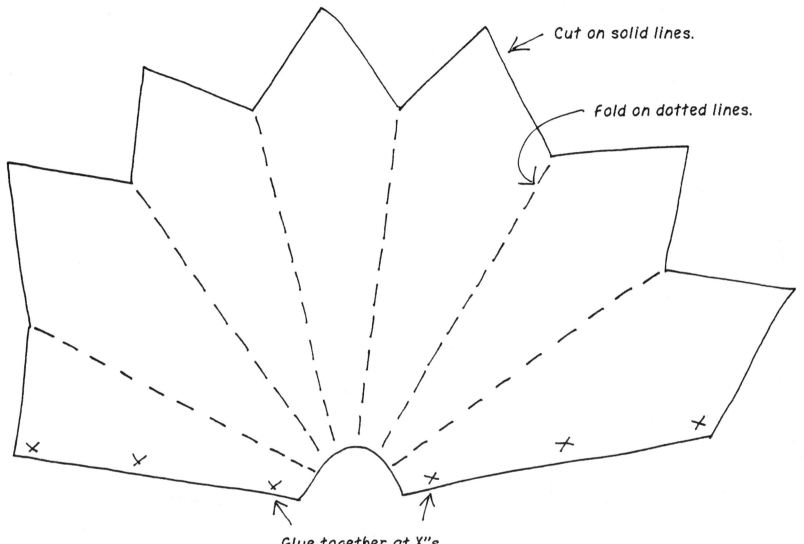

Cut on solid lines.

Fold on dotted lines.

Glue together at X"s

❀ MATERIALS ❀

Balloon*

String

White glue

Construction paper
the color of bird

Paper hole punch

Blow up the balloon and knot the end. Dip the string in white glue and wrap it around the inflated balloon. Continue wrapping, running the string over other wraps until the string begins to resemble the bars of a cage. Let dry. When the string is completely dry, pop the balloon, and pull the pieces out of the string cage.

Draw a bird on the colored paper and cut it out. Punch a hole in the top of the bird shape and hang it by a string inside the cage. Use another piece of string to hang the cage from a tack in the ceiling or on the patio.

*See warning, page 69.

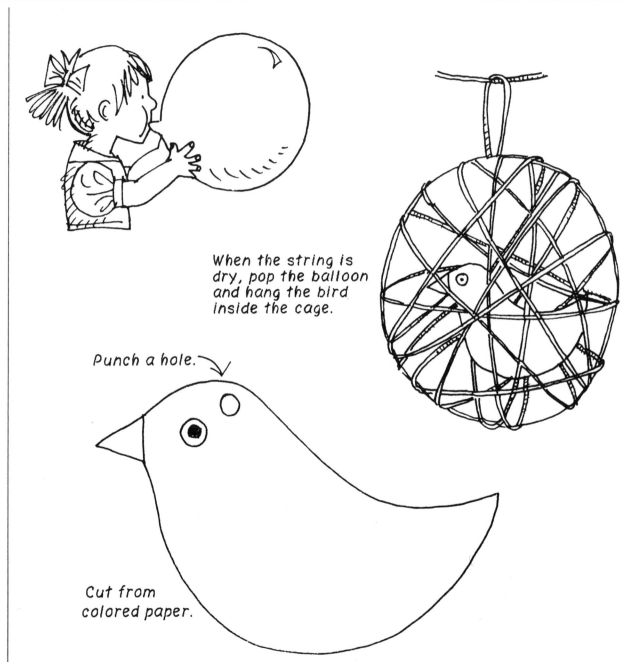

When the string is dry, pop the balloon and hang the bird inside the cage.

Punch a hole.

Cut from colored paper.

CRAYON CRAFT

Crayon Cookies

🌸 **MATERIALS** 🌸

Old pieces of crayons, broken up

Paper cupcake liners

Muffin tin

Warning: *Crayon wax can ignite at high temperatures, so be careful. Ask an adult to help, and use a double boiler.*
DO NOT EAT THESE "COOKIES."

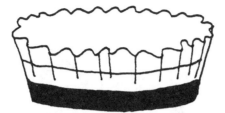

Layer different colors to make rainbow crayons.

Drop bits of crayon into the melted crayon wax.

Crayon Scratchboard

🌸 **MATERIALS** 🌸

Tagboard or lightweight cardboard, 8" x 10" or smaller

Crayons or crayon cookies (you just made those!)

Scratch tools: paper clip, nail, straight pin

Old crayons can be made into giant crayon cookies in different ways. You can melt all the similar colors together, then pour into the paper cupcake liners and cool. Different colors can be layered over one another, letting each layer cool before adding layers of another color, creating two and three colors in one cookie. Or, after the paper liner is about ½" full of melted crayon wax, drop in broken bits of unmelted crayon. They melt a bit and become part of the solid cookie when it cools.

Another method makes use of an oven. Chop the old crayons up into ¼" pieces and place in the bottom of paper cups. Place the cups in a muffin tin and put in a 400°F oven. Bake until the crayons just start to melt, about five minutes. Don't melt the crayons completely, or the colors will all mix to form one muddy color. Remove from the oven, and cool. Remove the paper when completely cooled. Crayon cookies are fun to use for leaf rubbings, or for scratchboard.

Color the entire piece of board with crayon, putting different colors in different areas. Color firmly, letting no white of the board show. The thicker you apply the crayon, the better your finished work will be. Color over the entire colored board with a black crayon. Color thickly, covering up all of the crayon color you just applied. Using scratch tools, scratch out a drawing. This is your chance to draw in lots of tiny details with your scratch tool. As the black crayon is scratched away, brilliant colored areas will peek out from beneath it. If you make a mistake while scratching your drawing in, just color over it again with the black crayon and scratch again.

❀ MATERIALS ❀

Light blue construction paper

Brown and green tempera paint
or markers

White glue

1 cup
popped popcorn

With brown paint or markers, draw a large tree branch on the blue paper. Add some green leaves. To create the fluffy apple blossoms, glue on pieces of white popped corn.

Draw a branch and leaves with paint. Glue popcorn down for blossoms.

❀ **MATERIALS** ❀

2 white paper plates

Colored markers or tempera paints and brush

Scissors

Stapler

Draw a large butterfly on the underside of one plate. Use paint or markers to color it in completely with bright designs. With scissors, cut the other paper plate in half. Trim away one inch from the cut edges of each half. Fold the plate with the butterfly on it in half. Crease down the center of the butterfly's body. Fold sides of the plate back toward the butterfly's body. Staple the cut plate halves to back side of the plate with the butterfly on it. Place plates so an opening is created along the crease of the colored plate. To operate the puppet, insert your thumb in one pocket, your fingers in the other. Close your hand and open it. The butterfly will flap its wings!

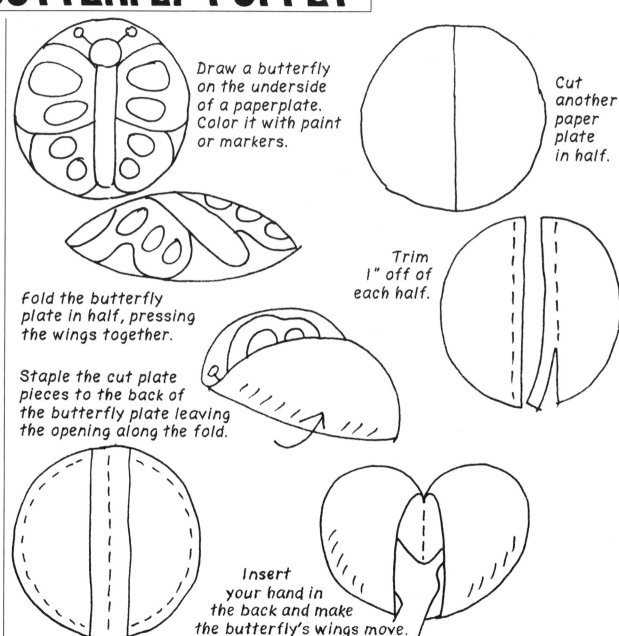

Draw a butterfly on the underside of a paperplate. Color it with paint or markers.

Cut another paper plate in half.

Fold the butterfly plate in half, pressing the wings together.

Trim 1" off of each half.

Staple the cut plate pieces to the back of the butterfly plate leaving the opening along the fold.

Insert your hand in the back and make the butterfly's wings move.

Take a wildflower walk, and bring along a thick telephone book or catalog. As you find pretty flowers you want to keep, lay each one gently on a page of the telephone book. (Be sure it is okay to pick them first. Some plants are endangered species or may be on private property.) Arrange the petals and leaves so they lie flat, and close the book. Skip about ten pages between flowers. Small blossoms dry best, but so do ferns and pretty leaves.

It takes between a week and a month for the flowers to dry completely. When dried, you can glue them to construction paper or mat board and frame. You can also glue them to paper to create unique greeting cards and stationery. After drying, some flowers lose their color. You can touch up the petals by delicately painting them with watercolors. Add a few drops of dish detergent to your paint water to help it adhere to the petals.

Another drying method works well if you have a whole bouquet of flowers. Gather the stems together and tie or bind with a rubber band. Then hang the bunch by the stems from a string. They can be tied to a clothesline, but should be hung indoors in a shed, garage, or attic and kept out of sunlight and dampness. They should be stiff and dry in about a week and a half. Arrange them in baskets or vases. Weeds, pods, strawflowers, statice and money plant dry well with this method.

You can also dry flowers by placing them in a borax and sand mixture. To 3 parts of borax, add 1 part heavy, clean, fine sand. Use a large container such as a cardboard box or wastebasket.

Pick the flowers by cutting them with long stems, using a knife or scissors. To cover them with the sand mixture, place some sand in the bottom of the container, and while holding the flower by the stem, gently pour the sand mixture around it until the blossom is submerged. It takes about three weeks for the blossom to dry. When dry, gently sift away the sand and remove the flower.

When you have enough flowers dried to make a bouquet, place the blossoms on stem wires by laying the wire next to the stem of the blossom. Wrap with green floral tape to secure the stem to the stem wire. When finished, you can spray the flowers with an acrylic spray finish if you want. This protects them against humidity.

Let the flowers hang upside down to dry.

Lay the dry blossom next to the stem wire and wrap with green tape.

PAPEL PICADO

May 5 is a big holiday in Mexico. On May 5, 1862, Mexican forces withstood French forces who were trying to take over Mexico for Napoleon. You can create Papel Picado and some paper bag pinatas to have a party of your own.

"Papel Picado" means "pierced paper" in Spanish and is created by skilled artists using layers of tissue paper and sharp instruments like nails to punch designs. The paper is used to decorate homes and shops in Mexico.

To create some for your own home, use brightly colored tissue paper. Cut a sheet into smaller sections and fold the sheet, smaller and smaller. Using sharp scissors, cut out designs along the folded edges. Cut small, geometric shapes. When the paper is unfolded, the cut designs will appear in interesting patterns.

To hang your papel picado, fold the top edge over a long piece of string. Fold the paper over about 1/2", and tape it securely. Add more pieces, until your string is full and tack it up across your room.

 MATERIALS

Colored tissue paper

Scissors

String or yarn if you want to hang your creations

PAPER BAG PINATA

 MATERIALS

Brown paper bag, lunch-size or larger

Several pieces of brightly colored tissue paper

String or yarn

Hole punch

Scissors

Glue

Cut the tissue into strips about 3" wide. Cut the strips into fringe, leaving about 1" uncut at the top edge. Starting at the bottom of the paper bag, glue the strips around the bag. Glue the next strip so that the fringe comes down and covers the glued area of the first strip. Layer the strips of fringe until the bag is covered. Cut several long streamers of various colors, and glue them to the sides and bottom, so they will hang and flutter.

With the hole punch, punch holes around the top of the bag, about 2" apart. Thread the yarn or string through the holes.

Fill the bag with candies or prizes. Pull the strings up securely and knot. Use the long string ends to tie your pinata where it can be hit with sticks. To break the pinata, Mexican children use sticks. Since your pinata will not be as hard to break as the ones you can buy in Mexico, you can make your own stick. Roll up a newspaper, taping securely with masking tape. Now, you are ready for the blindfold! Swat at the pinata and let your friends gather the goodies as they fall!

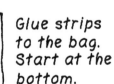

Fill with goodies and tie shut with the yarn. Hang up and start swinging.

Cut the tissue paper strips into fringe.

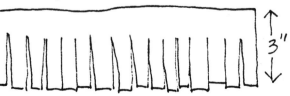

3"

Glue strips to the bag. Start at the bottom.

SUMMER FUN

 MATERIALS

9" x 12" piece of heavy cardboard (grocery boxes are perfect)

Vinyl adhesive-backed paper

Four spring-type wooden clothespins

Yarn, about 30" long

Scissors

Hole punch

Long and lazy summer days are just the time to try sketching outdoors. Make a clipboard to hold your paper and pencil.

Lay cardboard in center of adhesive-backed paper (sticky side up).

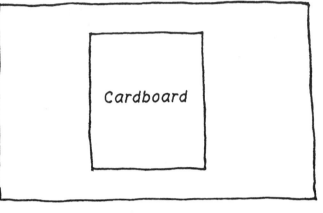

Cardboard

Cut a piece of adhesive paper large enough to cover the cardboard with extra on all edges for overlapping. The paper should be at least 20" wide and 14" long. Peel off the paper backing and lay the paper on the table with the sticky side up.

Use spring type clothespins to secure the paper to the clipboard for outdoor sketching.

Punch a hole and tie on a pencil with a length of yarn.

Place the cardboard in the center of the adhesive paper, fold the ends toward the center, overlap and smooth down the edges. Use the clothespins to hold down your drawing paper during outdoor sketching. If you want to use your clipboard for writing stories or letters, use a metal spring clip to hold the paper at the top of the clipboard. With the hole punch, punch a hole in the clipboard. Tie one end of the yarn piece through the hole. Tie the other end to your pencil.

Hula Skirt

 MATERIALS

Shredded computer paper from an office or bank; pieces should be about ¼" wide and about 2 feet long.

1"- wide masking tape

Scissors

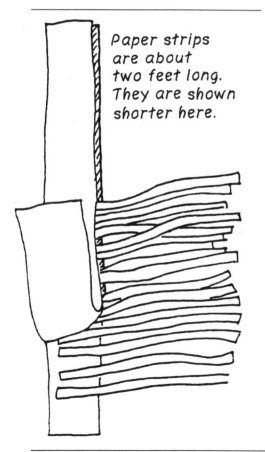

Paper strips are about two feet long. They are shown shorter here.

Warm summer days are the time for a little hula dancing. Create your own Hawaiian costume. Hula skirts are quick, cheap and fun. They can be tied on over your regular clothing.

You'll need to work on the floor for this one. Pile up some shredded paper to work from. Cut a strip of tape about 6" longer than your waist measurement. Lay the tape on the floor, sticky side up. Make the skirt by laying one end of the paper strips on top of the tape. Place the strips next to each other—the closer together, the more skirt to sway.

When the length of tape is full of paper strips, lay another piece of tape on top of the first one and press together to create a waistband. Wrap the skirt around your waist. Overlap and fasten with a large safety pin or more masking tape.

Every hula skirt needs a few leis to complete the outfit. Make a flower template out of cardboard or tagboard. Trace and cut out tissue paper flowers. Cutting through three layers of tissue at once goes faster. Punch a hole in the center of each flower.

Cut the straws into 1" long pieces. Cut a piece of string or yarn about 30" long.

String a straw piece first and knot the yarn around it, so the pieces won't fall off as you continue stringing.

String the straw pieces, putting three paper flowers between each section of straw. Knot the ends to create a long necklace.

Flower Leis

 MATERIALS

Drinking straws, 6 for each lei

Cardboard or tagboard, 5" x 5"

Colored tissue paper, small pieces in several colors

String or yarn, about 30"

Paper punch

Pencil

Scissors

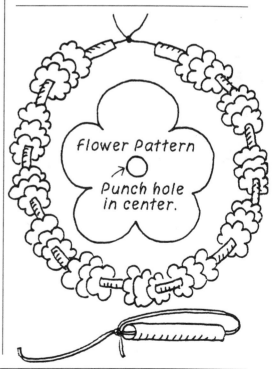

Flower Pattern

Punch hole in center.

If you like dancing, make some ribbon sticks to use while you move to the music. These are also super for pep rallies and parades. The colorful paper streamers will flutter and wave as you move them through the air.

Ribbon Sticks

 MATERIALS

Crepe paper streamers
Drinking straws
Stapler
Scissors

Cut three 36" paper streamers. You can use all one color or a variety. Holding the three ends together, wrap the crepe papers around the end of the straw, tucking the cut edges under. Staple to the straw.

Staple paper streamers to a straw.

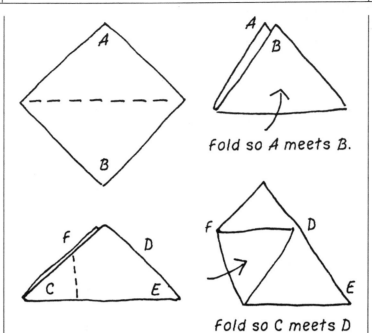

Fold so A meets B.

Fold so C meets D and E meets F.

With all that dancing, you'll work up a thirst. Create a paper cup like this for a drink of cool, fresh water.

Paper Cups

 MATERIALS

8" x 8" piece of paper

Fold the paper, so A and B meet.
    Then, fold, so C meets D.
    Fold E up to meet F.
    A and B are now the tips. Fold them down on each side.
    You can fill with water and drink up!

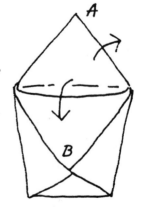

Fold A and B down—fill with water!

A DAY AT THE BEACH

Starfish

 MATERIALS

Posterboard

White glue

Yellow construction paper

Corn meal

Scissors

Pencil

Summer days make you think of the beach. With a few odds and ends you can take yourself away on a beach vacation, right at home!

Cut the posterboard and construction paper into identical star shapes. Glue together. Spread glue all over the yellow star. Sprinkle the corn meal into the wet glue. Shake off the excess corn meal when the glue has dried. Make several starfish in a variety of sizes.

Sailboat

MATERIALS

Plastic soda bottle

Sand or soil

Colored construction paper

Stapler

Tape

Scissors

Marking pens

Cut one from posterboard and one from yellow paper.

Experiment a little to find out how much sand you need to put into your bottle to keep it floating upright. If it tilts in the water, try adding a little more sand. Once upright, screw the lid on firmly.

Cut out boat and sail shapes from the construction paper and add details with marking pens. Staple the pieces around the bottles, and tape securely. Make several boats or a flotilla, and fill up the backyard wading pool. You might want to add a Mayflower, Noah's Ark, the Jolly Roger...maybe even the Titanic!

 ## MATERIALS

Colored posterboard
Elastic braid, 1/4" wide
Stapler
Scissors
Pencil
Colored markers

Use the patterns to trace and cut out a visor from the posterboard. Decorate with brightly colored markers.

Cut a piece of elastic about 10" long. Staple one end to the visor. Adjust it to fit your head snugly. Staple the other end to the visor. Trim away the extra elastic.

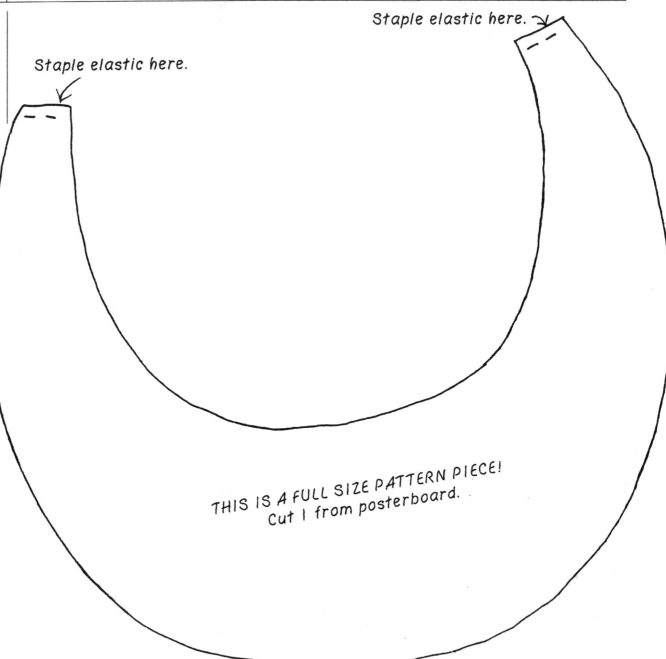

Staple elastic here.

Staple elastic here.

THIS IS A FULL SIZE PATTERN PIECE!
Cut 1 from posterboard.

What's a beach without palm trees? Make some of your own to decorate your room. If you have some clay dinosaurs, these palm trees help them feel right at home.

 MATERIALS

Toilet tissue tube

Green and brown construction paper

Glue

Scissors

Pencil

Black marker

Stapler

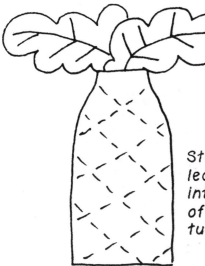

Staple leaves into top of the tube.

Trace and cut out two or three palm leaves from the green paper. With the marker, draw detail lines on the leaves. Cut a piece of brown paper to cover the tissue tube. Glue it around the tube. Draw a design with the pen to create the look of a palm tree's textured bark. Fold the tab down on the leaves and insert them into the end of the trunk. Pinch the trunk over the tabs and staple everything together. Staple twice to secure it.

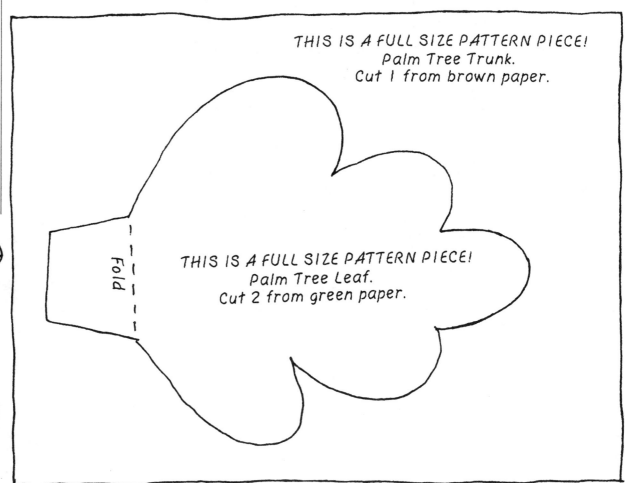

THIS IS *A FULL SIZE PATTERN PIECE!*
Palm Tree Trunk.
Cut 1 from brown paper.

Fold

THIS IS *A FULL SIZE PATTERN PIECE!*
Palm Tree Leaf.
Cut 2 from green paper.

Tourist shops at the beach often sell items made by layering colored sand into a container. You can use salt instead of sand and create a candle in its own holder. Layers of colored salt can be used to fill jars of all shapes and sizes, and used without wicks, too. If filled to the very top, they often hold the layered look for a long time and make handsome gifts.

 MATERIALS

Salt: about $1/3$ box for each candle

Empty baby food jar

Candle wick, about 2" long

Food coloring, various colors

Paraffin wax or candle wax

Empty can to melt wax in

Double boiler

Small bowl for each color of salt

Warning: Be careful, wax will catch fire if it gets too hot. Make sure an adult helps with the wax part of this project.

First, pour about $1/4$ cup of salt into each bowl. Squirt a few drops of food coloring into the salt—one color per bowl—and mix it well.

Pour the colored salt into the baby food jar, making each layer of color about $1/4$" to $1/2$" deep. Do not shake. Leave the top 1" of the jar unfilled.

Melt the wax carefully in a can placed in the top of a double boiler at low heat (both top and bottom of double boiler should have water in them).

Have an adult pour hot wax into the jar, over the top of the salt. Fill the jar almost to the top.

While the wax is still hot, and has not yet begun to set up, drop the piece of wick into the wax, letting about 1" of wick stick out at the top.

Let the candle cool undisturbed.

Wick was set down in the wax before it cooled.

← 1" of wax to the top of the jar.

← Layers of colored salt.

PLAY SKATEBOARD OR SCOOTER

MATERIALS

Popsicle sticks or tongue depressors

Plastic drinking straws

Glue

Scissors

Craft knife

Sand paper

Colored markers

Cut the Popsicle stick about 2" long. Sand the rough edges using sand paper or by rubbing against a cement sidewalk, rounding the cut edge to match the other end. Cut two sections of straw, both as wide as the Popsicle stick. Color the stick with markers. Glue the straw sections to the bottom of the board, to resemble wheels.

If you want to turn your board into a scooter, cut another section of drinking straw about 2" long. Cut a shorter piece, about 1" long. Glue the two to create a T-shape for the scooter handlebar. When dry, glue the handlebar section to the top of the board section. Hold in position until the glue dries.

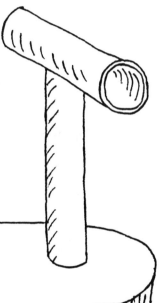

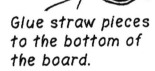

Glue straw pieces to the bottom of the board.

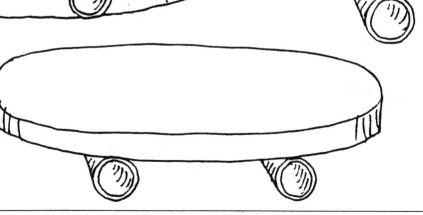

Glue straw pieces in place to create a scooter.

MATERIALS

Mat board

Foam core board

Craft knife

Masking tape

Pencil

Create a ramp for your play boards to do tricks and stunts.

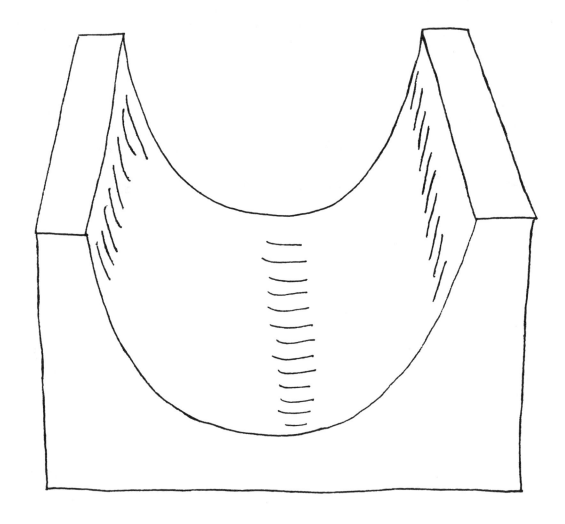

Using the diagrams, measure and cut out two end sections from the foam core board. Make them identical. Then cut out the two strips from foam core as well. Cut the rectangle from mat board or heavy poster board.

Curve and tape the rectangle to the curved sections, holding the board in place as you tape. Do one side, then form and tape the other. Tape the strips into place at the top to create platforms.

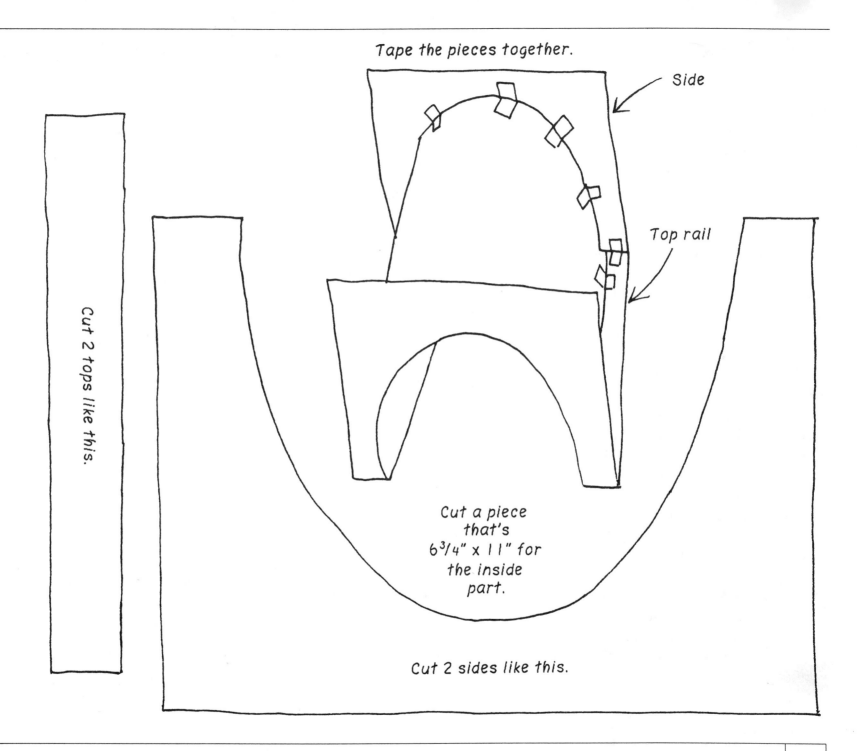

Tape the pieces together.

Side

Top rail

Cut 2 tops like this.

Cut a piece
that's
6³/₄" x 11" for
the inside
part.

Cut 2 sides like this.

maze and entertain your friends with the things you can make from balloons.

Clowning around with balloons is easy to do. The secret is in using balloons made especially for balloon sculpture. Look in your local phone directory for shops that carry party or magic supplies. The size professional clowns recommend is called #245 or #260-A, of the A series. These balloons are long, pencil shapes.

To sculpt, follow the diagrams. Inflate the balloon, leaving a portion uninflated. This allows the air in the balloon to expand as you create twists. Knot the end of the balloon.

Balloon shapes are created by forming bubbles in the balloon. The bubbles are held in place by a lock-twist to prevent the balloon from untwisting. A basic lock-twist is made by pinching the air out of a small area. Twist the two sections in opposite directions until they don't unwind when you let go.

See warning, page 69.

MATERIALS

Balloons, #245 or #260-A*

Markers

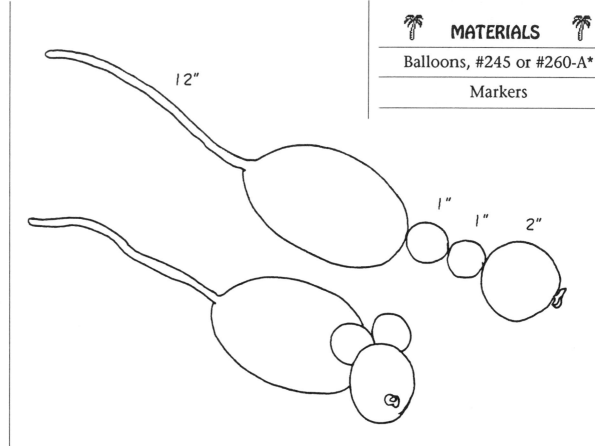

Mouse

Inflate the balloon until it's about 12" long. The uninflated section will be the tail. Knot the end.

Twist a 2" bubble, and two 1" bubbles.

Lock-twist the two 1" bubbles at the base to form the ears.

Swan

Inflate a balloon, leaving about 2" uninflated. Knot the end. Pinch off a 4" section next to the uninflated end. Twist this area with a bubble about 1" from the knotted end, until the two sections are locked.

Use a watercolor marker to gently dot on an eye.

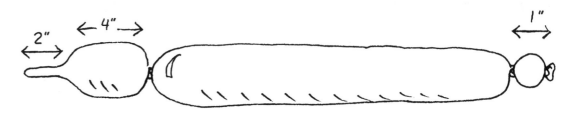

Twist together between the two bubbles.

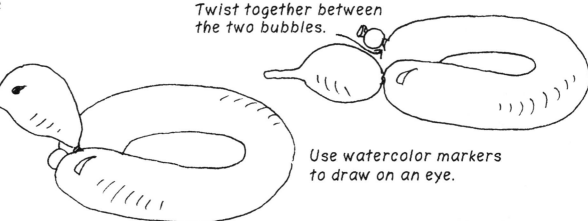

Use watercolor markers to draw on an eye.

Apple

To make an apple, you need to use a short balloon, with a colored tip. A red balloon with a green tip looks best. These can be purchased at party and clown supply shops.

Blow the balloon up, leaving 1" empty at the tip. Knot the end. Push the knot into the middle of the balloon until your fingers can pinch hold of it through the tip of the balloon. Pull the knot up and twist firmly. The twist around the knot becomes the stem.

green tip   red   Use a special "apple" balloon.

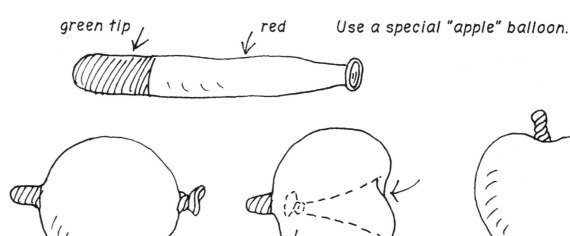

Blow it up, leaving the tip empty.

Push the knot through, and pull it up through the tip.

Twist tip around the knot to make a stem.

An old-fashioned project that always provides wonder and excitement is the crystal garden. Gather several small stones, or use barbecue briquettes. Either will work just fine. The bluing may be difficult to find. Look in the laundry supply section of grocery stores. It's in a small blue bottle, next to the starch and bleach products.

 MATERIALS

6-7 charcoal briquettes, or stones
Shallow bowl
6 tablespoons salt
6 tablespoons laundry bluing
6 tablespoons water
1 tablespoon ammonia
Food coloring

Put stones or charcoal briquettes in a shallow bowl.

Add the mixture and food colors.

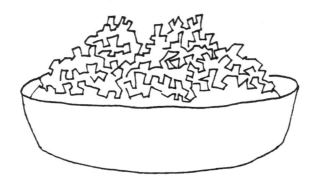

The garden will mysteriously grow.

Place the briquettes or stones in the bowl. Mix all the other ingredients together, except the food coloring. Pour the mixture over the stones with a spoon. You may have extra; just store it in a covered container and add to the garden over the next few days to keep it growing.

Drop food coloring over the coated stones.

Crystals will begin to form in about twenty minutes. Pour more solution and add more coloring every day, and the garden will continue to change and grow.

  MATERIALS

Copper wire
Rubber band
Marking pens
Small piece of red felt
Foam rubber strip, 2" x 36"

You can make your own clever walking snakes that are sold at fairs and carnivals. As you walk, hold the wire in your hand and guide the snake along the ground. The wire will not be very visible, so the snake appears to walk alone.

With scissors, trim the foam strip so it tapers to a point at one end. This will be the tail end.

Wrap the rubber band tightly around the other end, about 3" from the end. This will create a neck. Slip one end of the wire under the rubber band and twist it together firmly. With the snake on the floor and the wire in your hand, trim the wire, leaving 3" extra. Roll this 3" back and wrap it around itself to create a handle.

Decorate the snake with the markers, and he's ready for a walk.

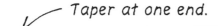

Taper at one end.

2" x 36" foam rubber

rubber band

Twist the wire to make a leash.

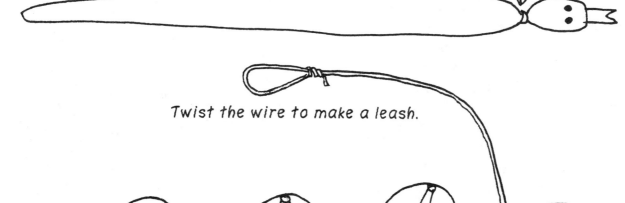

WALKING INVISIBLE DOG

 MATERIALS

Small dog collar

Sturdy wire

White glove

Another popular carnival toy is the invisible dog. All you need is a small dog collar and sturdy wire. If you have a leash, that's even better.

Soak the collar in white glue, shaping it while it's still wet so it will be round. Allow to dry. If you have a leather collar, it may not need stiffening.

Cut your wire so it will extend from your hand to about 5" from the floor. Add 3" for twisting the ends under.

If you are using a leash, insert the wire through the chains.

Fasten the wire to the collar by twisting it around the top and tucking the cut ends under so they can't be seen. Twist the other end of the wire and tuck the sharp edge inside, so you won't cut your hand. Gently shape the wire so it curves down a bit. Now when you walk your invisible dog, hold the wire in front of you as you walk, so the dog appears to be wearing the collar.

The best thing about the invisible dog is that she only needs to go out when you want to!

Since we're talking about dogs, you may want to make a doggie bank to save for a rainy day.

 ## MATERIALS

2 one-gallon milk jugs, with snap-on lids

Felt strip about 1" x 12", for the tail

Two pieces of felt, 6" x 8", for the ears

Felt strip, about 2" x 12", for the dog's collar

Hot glue gun

Two decorative eyes, about 1" in diameter (optional)

Black permanent marking pen

Position the milk jugs as shown. With the hot glue gun, glue the jugs together securely to create a head and body.

Use the glue gun to glue the eyes on both sides of the head.

Trim the 6" x 8" felt pieces so they are rounded on the corners, and slightly smaller at one end. These are the dog's ears.

Position them at the sides of the head, with the smaller end at the top. Use the glue gun to dot a line of glue across the top end of the ear. Press it into place on the dog's head.

The 2" x 12" felt strip is a collar for the dog and hides the glued neck area. Position it around the dog's neck, trim it to fit, and secure in place with the glue gun.

Use the black marker to color the jug's snap-on lid completely black. It is the nose. Snap it back on the jug. With the marker, draw a mouth on the front and side area of the dog's face.

Position and glue the long felt strip in place on the body, creating the dog's tail.

With a craft knife, slice a slit somewhere on the dog's back so you can insert coins. Ask an adult to help with this, because these jugs are slippery.

When you are ready to take money out of the bank, remove the lid from the back end of the dog, and shake it out.

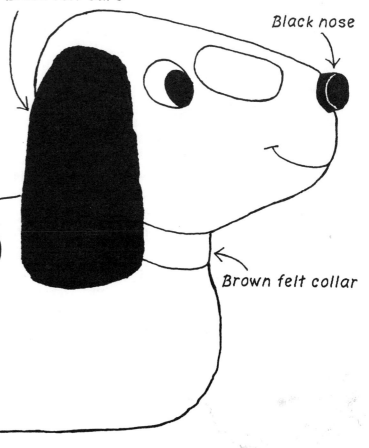

Black felt ears

Black nose

Tail

Brown felt collar

Slit for Money

 MATERIALS

Empty squeezable bottles

Flour

Salt

Water

Tempera paint

Paper

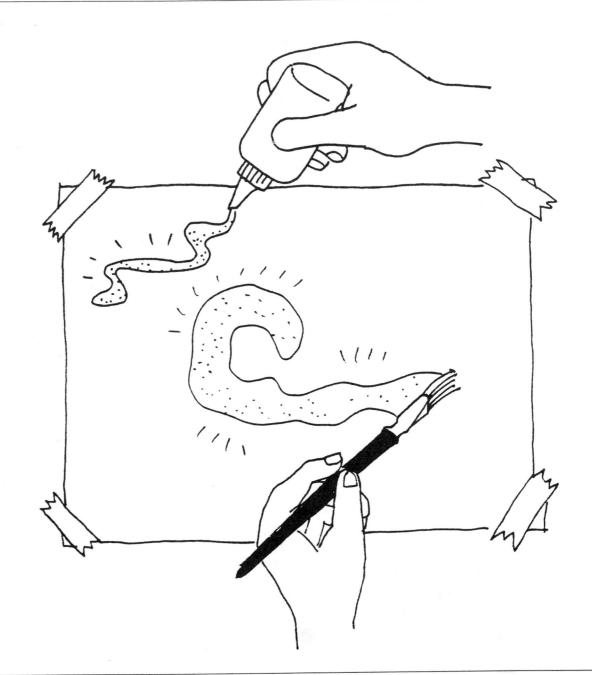

Mix equal parts of flour, water and salt. Pour some of the mixture in each squeeze bottle. Add tempera paint to each bottle and shake well.

Squeeze the paint onto paper, creating a design, word or picture.

Let dry. When the paint is dry, the salt makes the picture sparkle.

If you like, you can brush the paints on instead of squeezing them.

Bubble Fun

 MATERIALS

Liquid dish soap
(Joy® works best)

Water

Flat cake or pie tins.
Larger tins for large wands.

Thin wire

Heavy-duty scissors to cut the wire

Glycerin
(available at drug stores)

Mix up the dish soap, some water, and a spoonful of glycerin in a pan. You don't absolutely need the glycerin, but it makes the bubbles last longer and get larger without breaking.

Create your own wand, bending the wire into whatever shape you wish.

Dip in the soap solution, and wave in the air to create zillions of super bubbles.

Summer is for blowing giant soap bubbles. You can make your own bubble solution and create huge bubbles.

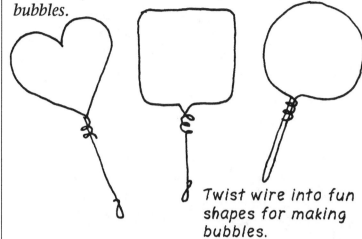

Twist wire into fun shapes for making bubbles.

Giant Soap Bubble Wand

Tie 48" of string between 2 plastic straws.

Want to create really huge ones? Of course you do! Use two drinking straws, and a length of string, about 48" long. Thread the string through both of the straws, and knot the ends. Lay the straws and string down in the soap solution. Gently lift up the straws, one in each hand. Spread the straws apart as you lift, and a giant bubble will form. Wave your arms across in the air, and it will be set free, to float up, up and away!

Bubble Art Notepaper

 MATERIALS

Tea cups or paper cups

Drinking straws

Dish soap

Water

Tempera paints

Typing paper

Cut the typing paper in half or fourths. Mix the soap and water in equal amounts. Add one color of tempera to each of the cups. Use the straw to blow air into the paint mixture until it bubbles and froths up. While the bubbles are still full, gently lay the paper surface over the bubbles. They will stick to the paper, then collapse. They will leave their colorful print on the paper.

Let dry. Then fold paper in half to create cards, stationery or gift wrap.

Marbleizing is a great way to create special stationery, and when you dip an ordinary pencil into the mixture, it will come out to match. Marbleizing creates a really beautiful pattern. The secret is in choosing colors that look nice together. You can use spray paint in the project, so it's a good way to use up all those odds and ends of spray paint in the garage. Or you can use oil-based house paint or artist's oil tube colors.

Work outdoors or in a well-ventilated area. Cover everything around you with the newspapers because this project can be messy. Oil paints do not wash off with water.

Fill bucket to about 2" from the top. If you are using spray paints, spray some paint onto the water for about 4-5 seconds. Add another color, overlapping the colors. If you use liquid oil paints, spoon or pour a few tablespoonfuls onto the water. If you are using oil tube paints, mix the paint to a creamy consistency with some turpentine,

Swirl paint around on top of the water. Lay paper down on the paint and it will stick to the paper.

Hang paper to dry.

Dip pencils in the paint and stick them in an egg carton to dry.

MATERIALS

Bucket of water
Oil-based paints
Wooden paint stirrer or stick
Newspapers spread out for a project drying area
Typing or construction paper
Pencils, for dipping

then drop by spoonfuls onto the water. Use the stick to spread the paint around on the top of the water and create interesting swirls, being careful not to mix the colors completely together.

Lay a piece of paper on the surface of the water. It will pick up the paint in its swirled design. When dipping pencils, hold by the eraser and roll the pencil over the surface of the water, picking up the paint as you roll.

Lay the paper on the newspapers and let dry. To let pencils dry, stick them into the bottom of empty egg cartons. It takes several hours to dry.

If you like, you can purchase a disposable aluminum roasting pan at the grocery store, and use it instead of the bucket. That way, you won't have to clean the oil paints out of the bucket when you are through. Just throw the roasting pan away or keep for another project.

AUTUMN ARTS

STAINED GLASS LEAF PICTURES

Colorful fall leaves
Waxed paper
Steam iron
Construction paper strips, 1" wide
Old newspaper
Glue or paste

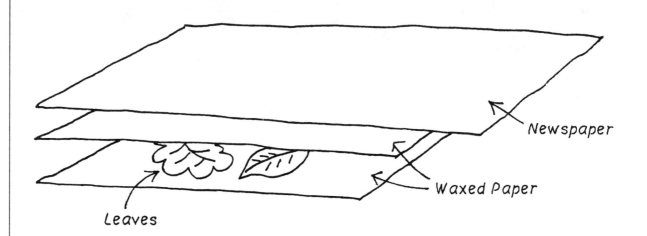

Newspaper

Waxed Paper

Leaves

Place a few leaves in an interesting arrangement between two pieces of waxed paper. Lay a piece of newspaper over the waxed paper. Press gently with a warm steam iron. The waxed paper melts together, sealing around the leaf. Trim the waxed paper edges with scissors, and glue the construction paper strips over the edges, creating a frame.

These "stained glass" pieces look nice taped on windows, so sunlight can shine through.

Glue paper strips to create a frame.

NATURE ART

Seed Mosaics

 MATERIALS

Piece of cardboard

White glue

Assorted tiny seeds: corn, bean, sunflower, fennel, dill, watermelon, squash, lentils, pearl barley, kidney beans; also seed pods from weeds, trees and bushes

It's easier to work with a wide variety of seeds and pods if you sort each seed type into its own paper cup or small bowl. Then take out only what you need so they won't get all mixed up. Start by spreading glue on a small area of the cardboard. Then set seeds into the glue in your own arrangement. You might want to create interesting patterns of shapes and colors, or create a scene using the natural color and texture of the seeds to express your ideas.

Indian Corn Collage

 MATERIALS

Tempera paint: orange, yellow and blue

Construction paper

Dried corn husks (from local gardeners or farmers, roadside stands, or purchase in craft store or Mexican food section of grocery store)

Glue

Draw an outline of a corn cob if you choose, or do the printing freehand. Use your finger to print kernels of corn by dipping your finger into the paint and pressing onto the paper. Keep changing colors without washing your finger, because Indian corn has blended colors. Press the paint spots in the shape of an ear of corn. When the paint dries, glue corn husks down so it looks more like a real ear of Indian corn. If you can't find corn husks, cut out and glue on husks made from crepe paper or construction paper.

APPLE PEOPLE

🍎 MATERIALS 🍎

Apple, peeled
Lemon juice and salt mixture
String, Popsicle stick or wire
Jar
Tempera or watercolor paints
Cloves, beads, seeds, corn for eyes and teeth
Pipe cleaners
Long-necked bottle
Cloth
Glue

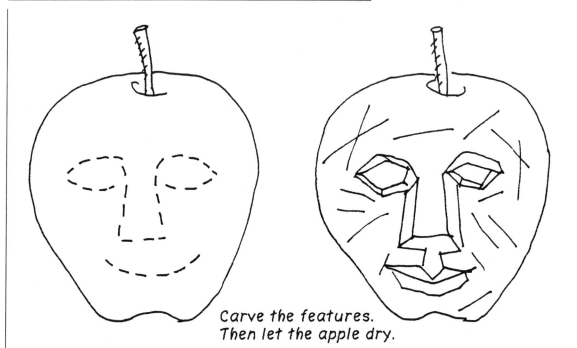

Carve the features.
Then let the apple dry.

Apples were a popular material that pioneers used to create dolls or interesting characters.

Use any kind of apple. Peel it carefully, keeping the surface as smooth as you can. Use a knife or spoon to carve the features. Because the apple will shrink and wrinkle up as it dries, the face will look different from the one you cut into the fresh apple. You may want to carve several apples, and pick out your favorite one later when they are all dry. Make a few cuts across the apple forehead to give wrinkled lines there.

When you have carved out a simple nose, mouth and eye sockets, paint the head with a mixture of lemon juice and salt to bleach the skin color.

You can attach a string to the stem to hang it or push a wire or Popsicle stick into the apple and let it stand in a short jar. Put in a warm place for three weeks.

When the head is dry, paint it with tempera or watercolors if you want, rouge the cheeks with a little powder blush makeup, or leave in its natural state.

You will have to stick something dark and round into the eye sockets for eyes. Use whole cloves, nails, beads, seeds or bead-topped straight pins.

A wire body can be bent into shape.

The mouth can show a row of teeth made by using seeds, corn, rice or tiny pearls, sticking or gluing them in place inside the mouth opening.

To make hands and feet, use apple slices and carve them a little. Let dry just like the head. You can also use pieces of felt for the hands.

For arms and legs, use pipe cleaners, wire or strips of twisted paper.

The body can be made from a long-necked bottle. When the head dries, glue it to the bottle. Then drape clothes over the bottle body.

You can also use wire for the body, shaping it like the drawing. Wrap strips of soft cloth over the wire to build up a body. Cut and glue cloth onto the body to create the clothing. Create a stand for your figure from a block of wood.

MATERIALS

Corn husks

Pipe cleaners

Pan of water for soaking husks

Dolls made from the husks of corn were made by pioneer and Indian children. Make your own with husks from your garden, a craft shop, or grocery store (check the Mexican food section). Soak the dry husks in water for five minutes. Tear some of the husks into long strips to be used later for tying bundles together.

Roll strips of husk into a ball and wrap in a rectangular piece of husk. Tie at the bottom for a neck.

Draw a face on it with a colored marker. Use corn silk or yarn for hair. Glue it to the doll's head.

Make a head. Draw a face with marker.

Roll and tie husks or roll a husk around a pipecleaner and tie.

Tie arms to head below the neck.

Tie body husks together at the waist.

Tie body to chest section at the neck. Fold the husks down to make a collar.

Arms can be made two ways:
1. Tightly roll a few long pieces of husk and tie with husk strips about ½" from each end to make a wrist and hand. Tie tightly again in the middle.
2. Cover a pipe cleaner by rolling a strip of husk around it. Then cover with a sheet of husk and tie the same as above.

After you have a finished arm section, tie it to the backbone at the neck level. Attach the arms to the head as in the drawing, binding the sections together with strips of husk.

A body is made by rolling 15–20 husks together and tying at the waist. The lower half should be slightly longer to look like a skirt.

Insert the head and arm section into the body, and tie at the neck.

To make a boy doll, make the legs the same way as the arms, and tie to the chest with strips of husk.

🍎 **MATERIALS** 🍎

Fabric pieces torn into strips

Needle and thread

You can make a real braided rug for your room. Use fabric pieces or old clothes torn into strips.

Cut or tear the fabric into strips that are 1" to 2" wide.

Sew three strips together at one end. Braid the three together. They don't have to be the same length, because as you get to the end of a strip, sew another one to it with needle and thread and keep on going.

When your braided piece gets to be about 3 feet long, start coiling it into a rug. Twist the braided strip around the end you started with, keeping it flat as you go, wrapping it around and around. Sometimes it's easier to start by twisting the beginning around a small piece of cardboard or a wad of paper. Sew the coil in place as you go with a heavy needle and

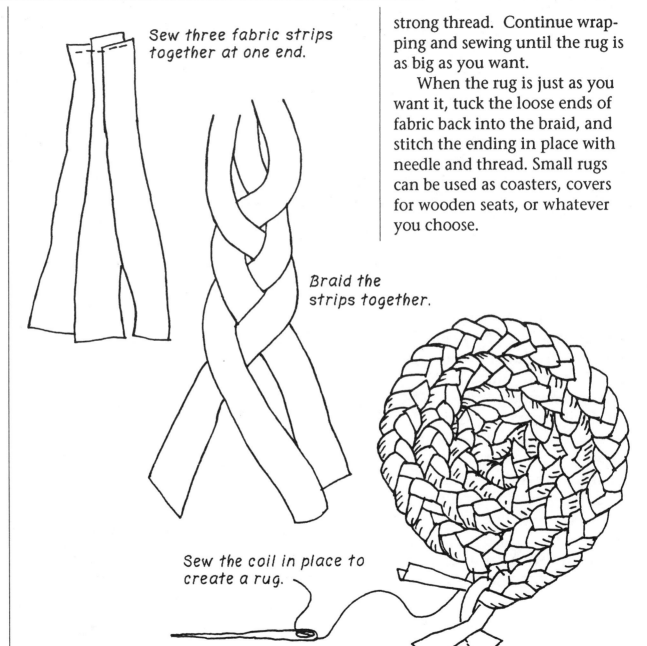

Sew *three fabric strips together at one end.*

Braid the strips together.

Sew *the coil in place to create a rug.*

strong thread. Continue wrapping and sewing until the rug is as big as you want.

When the rug is just as you want it, tuck the loose ends of fabric back into the braid, and stitch the ending in place with needle and thread. Small rugs can be used as coasters, covers for wooden seats, or whatever you choose.

MATERIALS

Oatmeal box (cylindrical shape)

Fabric or wallpaper scraps

Scissors

Glue

Make a cradle that really rocks for your doll or your sister's. You will need an oatmeal box, the kind that is shaped like a large tube. Cut it into a cradle shape, just like the drawing.

You can paint the cradle, but covering it with wallpaper scraps or fabric pieces is also fun. Use scissors to trim the fabric or paper to fit. Glue it in place. Add a little lace trim around the edges if you want or any decoration you like.

Extra fabric can be cut to line the inside of the box, too. If you have enough, cut some to make a matching blanket to keep the doll or teddy bear cozy.

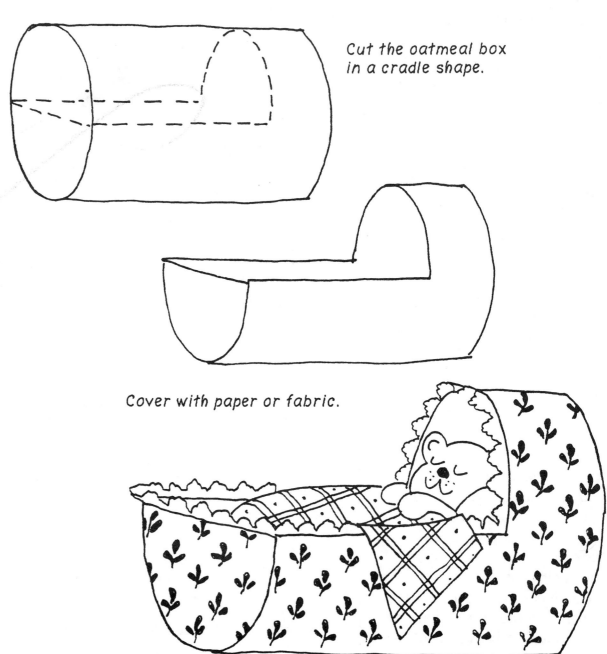

Cut the oatmeal box in a cradle shape.

Cover with paper or fabric.

MATERIALS

Seven 2$\frac{1}{2}$" x 3$\frac{1}{2}$" pieces of thin wood

Sandpaper

Twill tape (found in fabric departments)

Stapler or glue gun

These clatter blocks have been made for years. They are hard to figure out, but if you make them, you'll see the secret trick.

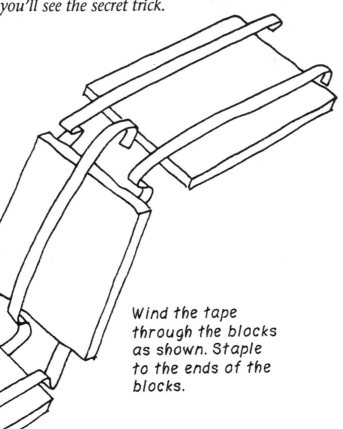

Wind the tape through the blocks as shown. Staple to the ends of the blocks.

Sand the wood pieces smooth. Attach the blocks to each other with the twill tape. Cut two pieces of twill tape 28$\frac{1}{2}$" long. Staple or glue the ends of the tape pieces to the edge of the first block. Space the two tape pieces 1$\frac{1}{2}$" apart.

Weave the tapes in and out between the blocks and then staple the ends to the bottom edge of the seventh block.

Weave a third piece of tape (21$\frac{1}{2}$" long) in and out of the blocks in the opposite direction. Staple or glue the ends to the inside edges of the first block and the last block.

To make Jacob's Ladder work, hold the second block and let the top block tumble down causing each block below to drop and tumble.

SCARY GHOSTS

Bean Ghosts

🍎 **MATERIALS** 🍎

White lima beans

Glue

Black permanent fine-tip
marker

Construction paper

Use construction paper to
create a ghostly scene: haunted
house with black paper, spooky
graveyard scene, or old gnarled
tree. Glue lima beans in place
on the scene, add eyes and
rounded "O" mouths. The beans
are the ghosts in your scary
scene.

Tissue Ghosts

🍎 **MATERIALS** 🍎

Tissues

Rubber band

This ghost project is one everyone tries sooner or later. Use
white tissues and a rubber
band. Wad up a tissue into a
round ball, lay it in the center
of another tissue. Wrap the
second tissue down around the
tissue ball and secure it with
the rubber band. Use a marker
to dot on eyes, and you have a
finished ghost!

Spiders

🍎 **MATERIALS** 🍎

Pompoms; 1 for each spider

4 pipe cleaners

Use black pompoms and black pipe cleaners to create spiders to perch everywhere.

Use four pipe cleaners. Tie them all together in the center, using half of another pipe cleaner twisted around them to hold them together. Spread the pipe cleaners apart a little, and fold the ends to create spider legs. Glue a pompom onto the center of the leg section. You can use a paper punch to punch out two red eyes, and glue them to the pompom.

If you want to create a web for your spider, string some black yarn across a doorway, back and forth, tying the pieces together here and there, using tape to fasten the pieces to the doorway.

Tie 4 pipe cleaners at the center. Fold to make legs.

Glue a black pompom to the legs. Stick on two paper eyes.

Spider Webs

🍎 **MATERIALS** 🍎

Black construction paper

White tempera paint

Cake pan

Marble

Cut a piece of black paper to fit in the bottom of the cake pan. Place half a spoonful of white paint in the middle of the paper. Drop a marble into the pan, and tilt it back and forth so the marble runs through the paint and leaves a trail of paint that looks like a spider web.

Paper Sack Pumpkins

Gauzy Ghosts

These are quick and fun to make.

MATERIALS

Brown paper lunch sacks

Orange and green tempera paint and brush

Rubber band

Old newspapers

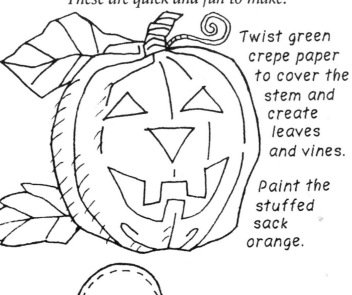

Twist green crepe paper to cover the stem and create leaves and vines.

Paint the stuffed sack orange.

MATERIALS

24" x 24" square of cheesecloth

Liquid starch

Glue-on craft eyes or make eyes from white and black felt pieces

Orange or rubber ball

Drinking glass

Two pencils

Tape

To make a paper bag pumpkin, stuff a paper sack with old crumpled newspapers. Gather the open top and crimp edges together. Close the sack with a rubber band to form a stem handle. Paint the sack orange, and the stem green. When the paint dries, turn the pumpkins into jack-o-lanterns by using black paint, markers or cutting out paper shapes and pasting on pumpkin for eyes and mouth.

Make a lot of these pumpkins and put them together to make a pumpkin patch. Use green crepe paper streamers to twist vines from the stem of each pumpkin. Group the pumpkins close together and twist leaves and tendrils from the crepe paper.

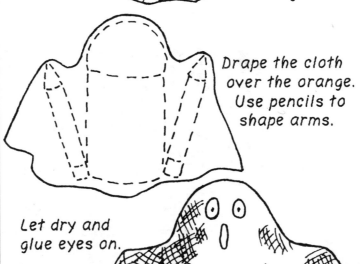

Drape the cloth over the orange. Use pencils to shape arms.

Let dry and glue eyes on.

Pour a cup of liquid starch into a small bowl. Dip the cheese-cloth in the starch until it's all wet. Set the orange on the top of a drinking glass. Gently drape the wet cheesecloth over the orange, bringing the edges down evenly all around. Use the two pencils to create arms for the ghost. While the starch is still wet, stick the pencils up and drape the fabric gently over them. Use tape to secure the pencils to the sides of the drinking glass, or to the table top.

Let the ghost dry. Glue on eyes.

MATERIALS

Brown paper lunch sack

Cardboard egg carton

Rug yarn for hair

Black construction paper

Two or three green split peas or lentils

Glue, scissors, pencil

With scissors, cut away the egg carton so that you have a section with two egg cups and the protruding divider section that goes between four egg cups.

Draw and cut out hat and dress shapes from the black paper.

Cut two small black circles for eyes, and glue them in the bottom of the egg cup sections.

Cut the yarn into several 6" sections and glue to the bag for hair. Glue the hat on top of the yarn.

Glue the dress to the bag. Glue the egg carton section to the bag. It will be the eyes and nose. Draw a wicked mouth on the bag.

Last touch—glue the lentils to the nose to become the witch's warts.

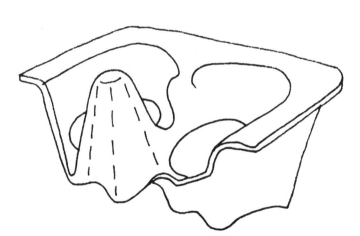

Trim 2 egg sections and the peak between them.

Don't forget to glue on a few lentil "warts".

🍎 MATERIALS 🍎

Milk cartons: the small half-pint size served in schools or any small boxes

Yogurt containers: the short, squat ones.

Drinking straws

Construction paper

White glue

Tempera paint

Liquid dish detergent

Pencil, scissors, paint brushes

Building a Pilgrim and Indian village is a nice way to get ready for Thanksgiving. For the base, you can use a table top covered with butcher paper, or tape down newspapers and paint them with tempera paint. If you use large pieces of cardboard for the base, you can glue the houses and trees in place, and the whole village will be movable.

Remove the staple from the top of the milk carton. Trim with scissors as shown in the drawing. Cut down from the top, to 1" below the folded edge of the carton at all four corners. On the sides with creases, trim off the corners diagonally, leaving a triangle flap on two sides. Fold the sides in and restaple at the roofline.

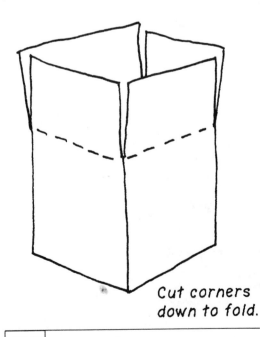

Cut corners down to fold.

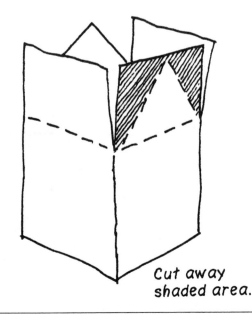

Cut away shaded area.

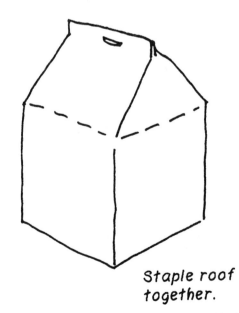

Staple roof together.

Add a squirt of detergent to the tempera paint, so the paint will adhere to the waxy surface of the cartons. Paint the cabins as desired. When they are dry, glue on paper doors, windows and details cut from construction paper or draw on with markers.

To make wigwams for the Indians, turn the yogurt containers upside down, and paint with tempera. When dry, spread with white glue and stick on pieces of dry grass and straw.

To make trees, cut two identical tree shapes from green construction paper. Cut a drinking straw in half, so it's about 4" long. Glue the straw between the tree shapes to serve as a trunk. Roll a ball of modeling clay, and push the end of the straw into it to stand the tree up.

To make bushes, tear green sponges into pieces and dab with splotches of tempera paint.

If you want to add people to your scene, use modeling clay or pipe cleaners and cut paper. Make some wild turkeys and deer, too. Use small twigs and rolled paper logs to create cooking fires. Let your imagination go!

Paint details on cabins.

Make wigwams from yogurt containers.

Glue a straw between 2 tree shapes. Stick the straw in modeling clay.

MATERIALS

Paraffin

Empty can

About 24" of candle wick

Saucepan

Create your own homemade dipped candles to use at the family's Thanksgiving table.

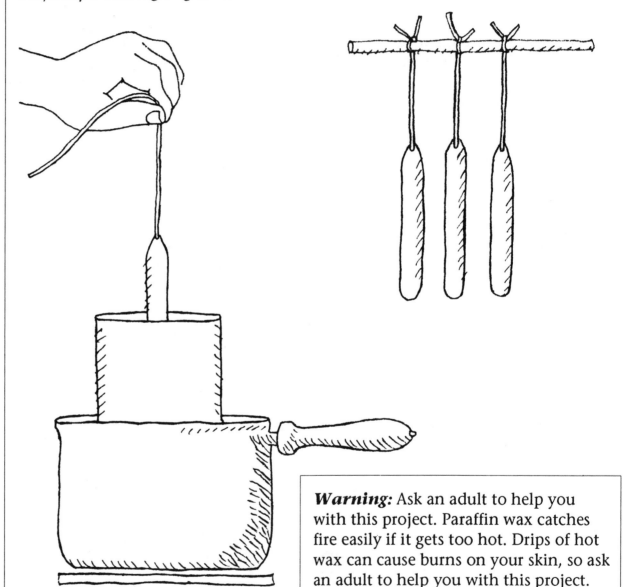

Fill the saucepan with about 2" water and heat it over low heat on the stove. Put the paraffin block into the can, and place the can in the water. The paraffin will melt slowly. Add another block of paraffin if you are making a very big candle.

When the wax is melted, lower the wick down into the liquid wax. Then slowly lift it out and hold it until the wax begins to cool and get solid. Then, lower the wick again, so more wax will coat it. Lift it up, and let it cool a little. Repeat this process, over and over, until the candle is the size you want. Then hang it by the wick end to cool. Trim the extra wick off when it is cooled.

Warning: Ask an adult to help you with this project. Paraffin wax catches fire easily if it gets too hot. Drips of hot wax can cause burns on your skin, so ask an adult to help you with this project.

WINTER WONDERS

Paper
Scissors
White tempera paint
Dish detergent
Toothpicks
Marshmallows

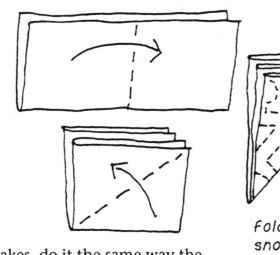

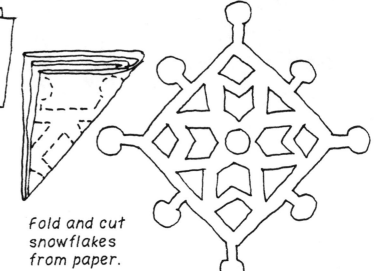

Fold and cut snowflakes from paper.

When you think of winter, you think of snow! You can make decorative snowflakes out of lots of things. Folded and cut paper snowflakes are as easy or as complicated as you want to make them. Just fold a piece of white paper several times. Then make a variety of cutouts along the folds. Open up the piece of paper, and it's a snowflake. Just like in nature, no two are the same.

If you want to decorate your windows with painted snow-flakes, do it the same way the window painters do for the holidays. Mix white tempera paint with a squirt of liquid dish detergent to make it easier to wash off the windows later. Use a paint brush and a corner of a sponge to dab on the white paint.

You can make snowflake decorations with toothpicks and miniature marshmallows. Insert toothpicks into marsh-mallows and connect to other toothpicks.

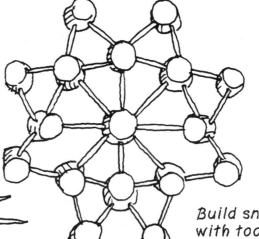

Build snowflakes with toothpicks and mini-marshmallows.

SNOW GLOBE PAPERWEIGHT

 ❄ **MATERIALS** ❄

Small jar with a lid
(a baby food jar is perfect)

Tiny toy or greenery

Epoxy cement

Moth flakes

Water

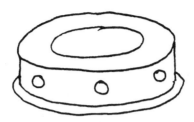

Make one of those fascinating old-fashioned snowstorms in a jar for yourself or to give as a gift.

Put something interesting in the jar. You may want to use a small toy such as a tiny snowman, or a tiny artificial pine cone and greenery. Use a hot glue gun to secure it to the bottom of the jar if you like. Fill the jar up to ¼" from the rim with water. Spoon in some moth flakes. Put epoxy cement around the rim of the jar and on the jar lid. Screw the jar lid on firmly and let dry completely. When the cement is dry, turn the jar upside down, and watch it snow!

> **Warning:**
> *Do not eat the moth flakes.*

Shake up a
snowstorm
in a jar.

❄ MATERIALS ❄

Coffee can lid

Green yarn in 18" lengths

12 red pony beads

24" piece of ribbon

Glue

Tape

Fishing line

Craft knife

Ask an adult to cut the center part out of the plastic lid, leaving a donut shape about 2" thick.

Wrap the green yarn around the lid, securing the ends to the back with glue or tape. As the lid is covered, string on a pony bead here and there to look like holly berries. Cover the whole lid with yarn. Then glue the yarn end to the lid, hiding it under the yarn wrapping.

Tie the ribbon into a bow and glue on at the top of the wreath.

Tie on a piece of fishing line, creating a loop for hanging from the Christmas tree.

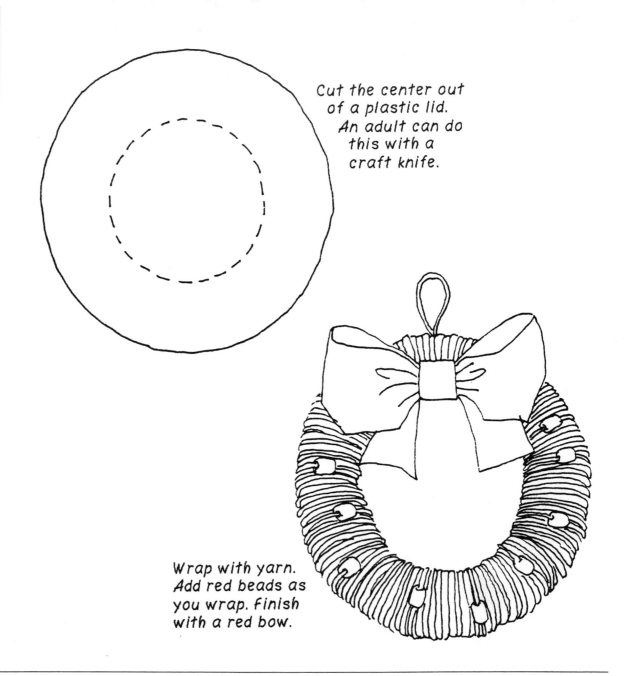

Cut the center out of a plastic lid. An adult can do this with a craft knife.

Wrap with yarn. Add red beads as you wrap. Finish with a red bow.

Animal Cracker Pins

❄ **MATERIALS** ❄

Animal cracker

Acrylic finish or clear nail polish

Jewelry pin back

Glue or hot glue gun

Make a fun and useful gift for someone you know. Paint an animal cracker cookie with clear acrylic finish or clear nail polish. When it's dry, paint the other side. Then, glue it to a jewelry pin back or a magnet.

Paint with clear nail polish.

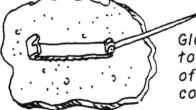

Glue pin to back of animal cookie.

Potpourri

❄ **MATERIALS** ❄

Rose petals, or any other fragrant flower

Herbs: Lemon verbena, marjoram, rosemary

Crushed orange peel (dried)

Cloves

Rose oil or lavender oil

Air dry the leaves and flower petals. This will take a few days. Use plenty of petals with a proportion of one cup petals to one tablespoon of herbs. In a large container, gently mix the ingredients with your hands. Add the oil a drop at a time mixing well after each addition. Store the potpourri sealed in jars. You may want to make a clay or papier-mache dish to hold your potpourri when you have it out to scent a room. Add another drop of oil to the potpourri when it begins to lose its lovely scent.

 MATERIALS ❄

Construction paper: white, light brown, dark brown, and red

Black marker

Hole punch

Glue

Cotton balls

Red pompom

Cut a 6" diameter circle from light brown paper. (Trace around a shortening can lid if you want.) Cut a 6" triangle from red paper. Cut antlers for the reindeer by spreading your hand out on the dark brown paper and tracing around it. Trace both hands. Cut out the tracings. Glue the triangle to the circle. Glue the horns so they stick out from behind the head.

Draw on the eyes and mouth with the marker. Use a paper punch to cut dots from the white paper. Glue the dots to the hat to decorate it. Glue the cotton balls to the hat.

Glue one red pompom in place for the nose.

❄ MATERIALS ❄

Clay of your choice
(see page 31; remember ceramic
clays must be fired)

9 small candles

Paint or glaze

Make a menorah to celebrate Hanukkah, the Jewish Festival of Lights. In December, Jewish children light a candle every day for 8 days. The candles are placed in a special holder called a menorah. Your menorah can be made in any shape you like. It must hold 9 candles—1 for each day of the holiday, and 1 for the candle used for lighting the other candles, called a shammes or leader.

Shape the clay as you like, flattening the base so it will stand solidly. Insert the candles (birthday candles or special Hanukkah candles) into the clay, pressing an opening a bit larger than the candle. Clays shrink as they dry so be sure to leave space or the candles won't fit. When dry either bake or fire, depending upon your clay type. Then paint or glaze to finish.

Every night of Hanukkah add a candle to the menorah.

*Make yours in any shape as long as there
are 8 candles and one to light with.*

CHRISTMAS TREE TRINKETS

Paper Christmas Balls

 MATERIALS

Heavy paper (old Christmas cards are great for this)

White glue

Scissors

Yarn or ribbon, about 6 " long

Trace 2" circles around a jar lid or similar round item. Trace and cut out 20 circles.

Fold each circle into a triangle, by folding the edges toward the middle in three places.

Make the ball by gluing ten circles together in a strip to make the middle of the ball. Glue this strip to make a circle. Add circles to the center band, creating the top and bottom of the ball. As you glue, hold the edges together or clip with paper clips until dry to keep the ball from coming apart.

When the ball is finished and dry, glue a loop of yarn or ribbon at the top for hanging.

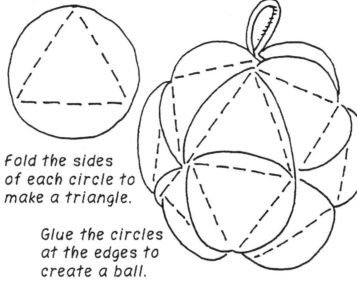

Fold the sides of each circle to make a triangle.

Glue the circles at the edges to create a ball.

Winter Bells

 MATERIALS

Egg carton

Aluminum foil

Yarn, about 10"

Scissors

Cut the carton sections apart and trim away the rough edges. Wrap the carton piece with aluminum foil, keeping the shiny side out. Smooth it firmly all over. With the point of the scissors, or a sharp pencil point, poke a hole in the top of the bell. Cut a piece of yarn about 4" long. Insert one end of the yarn down into the bell. Knot that end. Wrap the knot in aluminum foil, crushing it into a ball shape. You can make several bells and tie them in bunches, or tie single bells to tree branches with the yarn end.

 ❄ **MATERIALS** ❄

6 Popsicle sticks

Glue or glue gun

Paint or markers

Photo

Glue the Popsicle sticks into position to make two separate triangles as shown. Lay one triangle on top of the other to form a star. Glue together. Trim your photograph to fit the inside of the star and glue in place. If you want to hang, attach yarn or a ribbon at the top.

   This is an easy and treasured holiday gift that even the youngest hands can make.

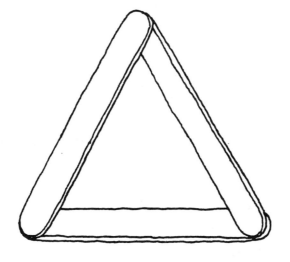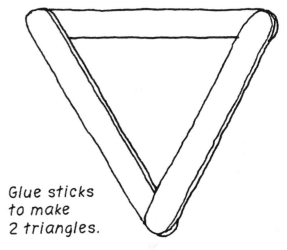

Glue sticks to make 2 triangles.

Glue one triangle on top of the other.

Glue a photo in the center.

CAROLERS

Thick magazine,
like a *Reader's Digest*

Papier-mache for caroler's head
(see page 70.)

Newspaper for head mold

Old socks

Small pieces of colored
construction paper: red,
black, white

Red spray paint

Tempera paint

This is a good project for making any standing figure—simply dress your figure in appropriate attire and add skis or a violin or a bouquet of flowers. These people are fun to make and to give.

Fold the page corners to the middle.

Begin by making the caroler's body. Fold each page of the magazine down as shown in the diagram. Continue folding until the whole magazine is folded. Sit the body up on old newspapers, and spray with red spray paint. Give it a couple of coats, so it is completely covered. Even out the pages before you spray, so the body looks the same all around.

To form the caroler's head see the section on papier-mache, making enough to completely cover a small wad of newspaper. Let the head dry completely. Glue the papier-mache head to the top of the body. A glue gun works very well for this.

Cut out eyes and mouth and mittens from the construction paper. Glue the features in place on the head.

Cut out a music book from colored paper. Glue the mitten shapes in place on the book. Glue the book and mittens in place on the front of the body.

Cut the cuff off an old sock. Fold the raw edges to the inside and turn the cuff edge back to create a stocking cap. Glue it in place on the caroler's head.

Use the rest of the sock to cut a long strip to wrap around the caroler's neck for a muffler.

❄ MATERIALS ❄

Colored felt pieces, 12" x 12"

White glue

Scissors

Sequins, buttons,
decorative trim

Yarn

Cut the felt square into two pieces, 6" x 12" each. Lay a 18" long piece of yarn along one of the 6" edges, placing it $1/2$" from the cut edge of the felt. Squirt a line of glue along the edge of the felt, and fold it back to cover the yarn. Press in place. Let dry.

With scissors, trim off the corners of the bottom of the banner, so it comes to a point.

Cut out shapes from other felt pieces, and glue them in place. Tie the yarn in a bow at the top and hang on the wall. Add decorations of your choice.

6"

Glue felt edge
down over yarn.

12"

Trim off corners.

These houses look just like ginger-bread houses, but are not as hard to make. They brighten up any deep winter day!

 ❄ **MATERIALS** ❄

Graham crackers, six squares for each house

Milk cartons, ½ pint size, washed and dried

Frosting (see next page)

Assorted small candies for decorating the house

Multicolored miniature marshmallows

Dry cereal in assorted shapes

Ice cream cone, the pyramid-shaped sugar cone type

Sturdy paper plate for each house

Prepare the frosting ahead of time, and keep it covered in the refrigerator (it will keep for up to five days).

To begin, dab a tablespoonful of frosting on the bottom of the milk carton, and stick it firmly in place in the middle of the paper plate. The icing acts as a glue and keeps the house from sliding around on the plate. Then, dab a tablespoonful or so of frosting on the back of each of four square crackers. Press them in place against the four sides of the carton.

The roof is the tricky part: Dab about two tablespoonfuls of frosting on the backs of two square crackers. Gently position the crackers on top of the carton, holding them in place to create the roof. It works best if you hold them in place for a minute or so, until the frosting dries a little. Also, if your frosting is too thin, the roof pieces may slide down. Add more powdered sugar to stiffen the frosting.

To cover the eaves at the front and back of the house, a small rectangle of cracker can be broken into a triangular shape and attached with frosting. To make it easier for young children, an adult can cover this eave area with frosting, hiding the carton there completely.

Now, the house is ready to decorate! Place candy, cereal or marshmallows onto the frosting before it dries. Spread the roof with frosting and place marshmallows or cereal pieces onto it in rows. Sprinkle powdered sugar over the roof to look like a skiff of snow is on the roof. Icicles of

frosting can be draped down from the roofline with a spoon. Candies and cereals can be used to create a path, door, chimney and windows.

To create a beautiful tree for the birds in the front yard, turn a sugar cone upside down and cover it with green frosting. Stick seeds, beans, peas, cereals or little candies all over it.

Little graham cracker bears or gummy bears might stand in front of the house. Dab some frosting on their bases, to securely glue them in place.

These little houses make yummy treats. If you want to save yours, wrap very tightly.

Frosting Recipe

1 pound confectioners' sugar
3 egg whites at room temperature
1/2 teaspoon of cream of tartar

Mix in a large bowl with an electric mixer at low speed. Increase the speed to high and beat for about seven minutes, until the frosting stands in stiff peaks when a knife is pulled through it. This makes about two cups of frosting. When making the houses, you will need about 1 cup for each house. Keep this frosting covered at all times, as it dries out quickly. Once dry, it is very hard and keeps the houses and decorations put together for years, if you want to save them.

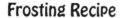

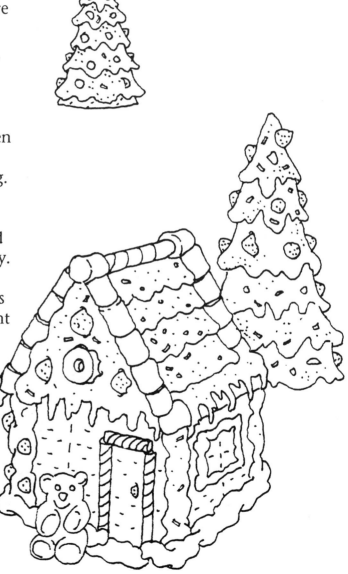

CHRISTMAS CANDLE DECORATION

 MATERIALS

Toilet tissue tube

Construction paper: white, yellow, green, red

White glue

Cover the tissue tube with white paper. Glue. Cut out two flame shapes from the yellow paper. Glue them to an open end of the tube, facing each other. Cut out nine holly leaf shapes from the green paper and nine red berries from the red paper. Glue the base of each leaf to the bottom of the candle, overlapping leaves slightly as you go around. Glue a red berry to the base of each leaf.

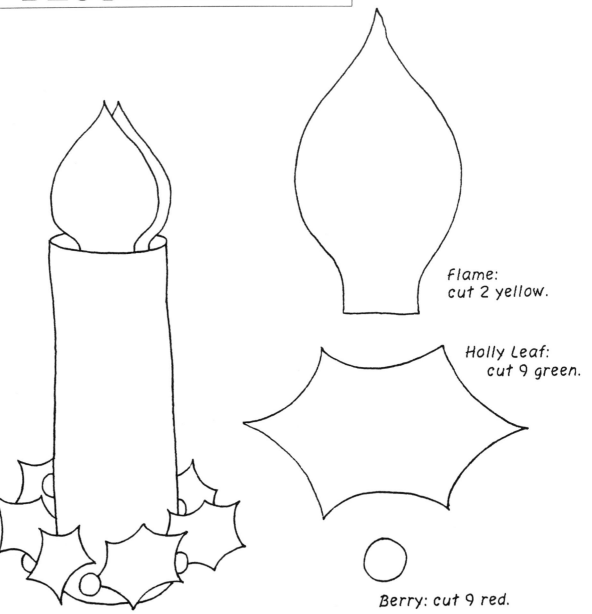

Flame: cut 2 yellow.

Holly Leaf: cut 9 green.

Berry: cut 9 red.

❄ **MATERIALS** ❄

| Aluminum pie plates |
| Nail and hammer |
| Heavy cardboard |
| Paper |
| Marker |
| Tape |

Place the cardboard on the tabletop to protect the surface as you hammer on the aluminum.

Draw a design on the paper with a marker. Tape the paper to the pie plate. Use the nail to punch out the design.

To hang, use a glue gun to attach a soda can pop-top ring to the back of the plate.

If you want to make your hanging even fancier, glue lace trim around the edge. Tie a fabric bow and glue it on, too.

❄ MATERIALS ❄

Lightweight cardboard or tagboard about 5" x 5"

2 rubber bands

Markers

Scissors

Hole punch

Make a spinner that reveals a message as it unwinds. You write half of your message on one side, the other half on the back; as it spins the message blends together right before your eyes!

Cut a circle about 3" in diameter from the tagboard. Use a jar lid or a drinking glass for a template if you wish. Punch two holes as shown.

Write the first half of your message on one side of the circle. Write the other half on the back of the circle, *upside down*. Loop the rubber bands through the holes and pull to secure.

To spin the message, slip your index fingers through the rubber bands and wind tightly. Spread your hands apart to let your message spin into view.

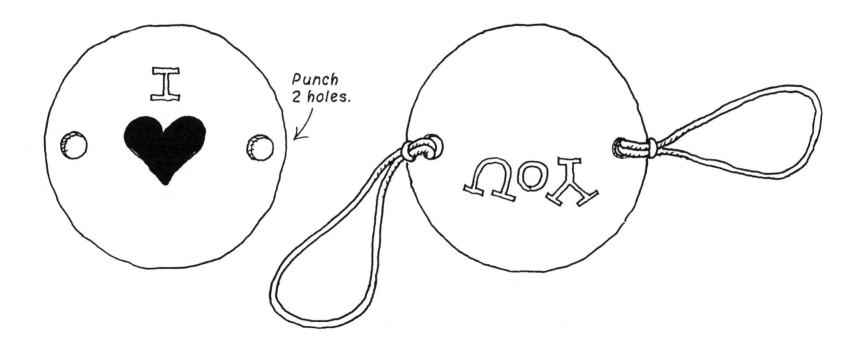

Punch 2 holes.

Stages in Children's Art

Children are ready to try new craft techniques and projects at various stages, just as they are ready for learning to read or write at a particular time in their own development. And, as with academic skills, children first need exposure to and experimentation with the materials, before they are ready to turn out finished products.

Most 4-year-olds aren't ready for projects that require long periods of time or precise cutting. Knowing what to expect from children in each developmental stage often helps determine which projects they want to do, as well as which projects they are apt to feel proud of and successful about accomplishing.

Today most educators follow the child development philosophy of psychologist, Jean Piaget, who proposed that there are various stages, or levels, through which children advance as they mature and develop more sophisticated thinking and motor skills. The following levels and suggestions for doing art and crafts with children are loosely fashioned

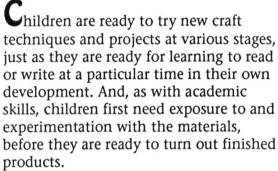

after his stages. The ages are merely general time frames; every child develops at the pace most comfortable for him or her.

The Preoperational Stage: About 4 to 7-Years-Old

Children at this level have difficulty observing more than one object at a time. Typically when pasting or drawing, they are likely to paste or draw one object next to another, rather than overlapping.

When working with these children, use language as you work to help them understand what is going on. Name each object, tool or material you are working with and talk about what you are doing. Children at this stage want to manipulate materials: fingerpaint, clay, or anything that is "hands-on" is a favorite for them. They usually can make an outline, and then fill it in. They are quite capable of drawing a picture and coloring it in. They don't need coloring books which are apt to stifle creativity and spontaneity.

Colors, shapes and patterns capture their interest, and most children don't relate colors to the natural world. Trees may have a red trunk and blue leaves which is just fine. Offer lots of bright colors in materials, but not just primary colors as children are fascinated with the wide range that exists. Just sit with a child and a crayon box with many different shades. Children usually want to use them all, and want to know what each is named. Rather than limiting the child's palette always add some interesting pastels or unusual color mixes, like turquoise or magenta, pronouncing the name as you introduce new colors.

Short attention span and limited motor control at this age mean that the sessions and projects are best when quick and easy. Children at any age have trouble sitting around waiting for something to happen, so have supplies and work space ready to go. Many children work on something for about

15 minutes and then they grow bored and restless, or they begin to overwork the project and become dissatisfied with it. Cutting accurately with scissors and tracing around a shape may prove difficult with their limited motor skills. They do, however, need to practice those skills. Give them ample time, provide extra materials so they can start over if they want to, and help before anyone becomes frustrated.

Keep supplies of tape, staples and glue handy. Most children do a lot of patching together as frequently portions of a project are accidentally cut away or parts fall off. Don't guard these supplies or comment on amounts used. Keep them available for the children to use as they need them. If you want to prevent waste, show how to operate the tape dispenser and how to pull the tape across the cutting edge. It is surprising how many young children have never been given a chance to cut a piece of tape for themselves!

Children in the 4 to 7 age group can work individually, or in large or small groups, depending upon what is being done. They learn by watching others. When preparing projects for them, keep in mind that an example helps them see what they are attempting to do with the materials they are given. Better yet, prepare several completely different samples, suggesting that there is no one way to do this. The samples should be put away as materials are handed out, before they begin their work. Kids are skillful at copying and want to please

adults, so their first response is to recreate your work, rather than use their own ideas and interpretations. Encourage expression of their own ideas. Discuss various possibilities and praise all their efforts. Try to have them envision what they think they want to make, and then encourage flexibility along the way. Conversation helps the children express their own ideas. Decision-making (to get started) and thinking about possibilities starts the creative thinking process. It is this process which children need to practice, rather than specific practice at "artistic" skills.

During this phase, children are at their most creative. They are usually pleased with their finished projects and don't really seem to care about what their peers think. Adults working with these children will enjoy the variety and excitement the children bring to their crafts projects.

The Concrete Operations Stage: About 7- to 11-Years-Old

Children at the Concrete Operations stage are capable of showing perspective and dimension in their drawings. They want to draw, paint or model in an imitative way. When given an object to duplicate from reality, such as painting a goldfish while sitting in front of a fish bowl, they draw what they know, rather than what they see before them.

In about the fourth grade, children's creativity may begin to slump. They seem to be concerned with realism in depicting things, as well as in the use of color. Children begin to look at spatial concepts. They can draw an object from various angles and show dimension. They understand and use techniques of overlapping.

Fine motor skills are well-developed and children are able to do finely detailed work, manipulating a variety of materials in weaving and sculpture.

In about the sixth grade, children's creativity drops further. They spend their time drawing pictures of the same things over and over, striving for more realism. Their lines tend to be sharp and angular. To counteract this, supply them with a variety of media and techniques. Begin to use an abstract approach to art and craft with them, rather than the stifling realism they tend to fall into. Show them that art is relevant to life: create unique sets of playing cards, dice, decorative paint and design themes for cars, industrial design, or fashion design. Help them

branch out by stretching the limits of what they know.

These pre-teens are very peer oriented. Those who can reproduce popular cartoon characters or other commercial designs receive recognition from their peers; those who are innovative are not similarly rewarded. As a group, pre-teens are trying to identify with each other and the larger group in general. Adults are frustrated when working with this age group, because these children often refuse to try anything different. In their quest for positive self-esteem, they lose the confidence to think creatively and imaginatively. If they decide they just want to depict the California Raisins accurately, provide the materials and instruction for them to be able to do that. Keep creative thinking alive by discussing other ideas. When ready, they will have the courage to experiment a little.

At all ages, children's work with three-dimensional media such as clay mirrors their work with two-dimensional art forms such as drawing. Thus, children in the first grade who draw people with legs sticking out of a big head will

also portray people in that manner using clay. As they begin to incorporate details into their work in one medium, they will do the same in all mediums they are introduced to.

Process vs. Product: Creative Expression vs. Results

When working with children and art, one must face a perhaps unspoken dilemma: our own ego and reputation become entwined with the child's finished product. What will others say about our skill, if the finished product is messy, distorted, or simply not "cute"? Frankly, for many adults, it takes a lot of self-control and a good amount of self-confidence to simply let children do their own thing. If you are tempted to do all the cutting and pasting for the child so it turns out "right," stop and ask yourself: What message am I communicating to this child at this moment?

Try to avoid using pre-cut or pre-dittoed cut-and-paste projects with children. These allow for little variation in finished products. The children's

finished products may appear "cute" to some adults, and they definitely save time, money (wasted supplies) and adult nerves, but they seriously fail the children. The real catalyst in a successfully creative crafts session for children is an adult who presents the materials, demonstrates some techniques, helps begin to generate some ideas, and then lets the kids go with it.

Encourage the freedom to deviate from the rest of the group, by coming up with their own interpretations. Let them learn from their own experimentation and that of those working around them. If Megan tried mixing all the colors together, and the result was mud, she may need to try again to achieve what she had in mind. Meanwhile, those working around her learned a little from watching her trials, and when they try using color in their own ways, they may or may not choose to duplicate her efforts. Again, allow enough time and extra materials for children who decide to start over on their projects. Adults often have false starts and work on refinements along the way in many types of endeavors. Children should have the same freedoms as well.

At all times, the process of creation is more important than the end product. Children learn techniques, skills and attitudes along the way. Most importantly they make choices for themselves, developing individuality and self-esteem.

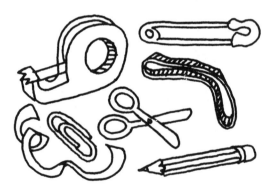

Working With Larger Groups

When it comes to art and craft projects, kids seem to quickly multiply, so that if you start with one child, very soon there is a whole group of interested children anxiously waiting to get into the act. These days, with preschool play groups, parents helping other parents by tending their children, the need for volunteers to run scout troops and to help out in preschools and elementary schools, all of these adults —parents, care-givers and teachers alike— can benefit from tips on working with larger groups.

There are fewer jobs more demanding or more rewarding than working with children, as anyone who does so regularly can confirm! There must be a special place in heaven, however, for those who face the challenge of working with children during an arts and crafts session! You need the stamina, speed, and footwork of an NFL player, as well as the quick reflexes, eyesight and steadiness of nerve of a gymnast. Adults may crumble and dissolve into tears, faced with those chubby hands reaching for the tempera paint all at once. Others have hidden in the closet, rather than face helping wild 10-year-old boys during a papier-mache session. But, if you are interested in both children and making things—enough to be using this book—then you must be made of the Right Stuff!

Attitude is the main tool you need before embarking on a creative project with children. Realize that spills happen, arguments occur, things drip and fall apart, and no one ever cleans up well enough afterwards. Once you see the excitement and pride on a child's face when a creation is completed, however, you'll be glad you were a part of it.

Clean Up

Let's get right to the problem area first. Clean up. It must be done. Someone must do it. Children are much like adults in this area. Visit an adult art class to see the similarities. Just ask any college-level art/craft instructor what the floor and sink look like after class. (I am convinced that these instructors don't have time to achieve great recognition for their own creative work, because they spend so much time cleaning up after the adults they have in class.) At least the people you and I work with have an excuse. They can't quite reach the sink!

Cleaning up has little appeal for any age group. Children can't seem to see that anything needs cleaning up and adults are either "late for an appointment," or "too tired." When I taught home economics, I was always rewashing the dishes in the classroom kitchen. As an art teacher, I find I am the only one who sees the paint on the floor or that the sink is stopped up. I don't say this to excuse children from participating in cleaning up after a session. Only to remind you that they are simply younger and modeling after the adults around them.

Don't feel guilty about offering motivators to children. Offering a reward or prize for getting the clean-up job done usually works wonders. Create contests between several children or groups. Offer a prize for the cleanest work space. This makes everyone responsible, rather than the one obedient child. It gives children a chance to work together, with their friends, sharing a common task.

Setting a time limit helps speed things up. I use a kitchen timer, letting the kids know when I start it.

Limiting Time on Task

Time limits and creativity don't seem to mix, yet we do live in a very practical world. Children who work slowly sometimes are not finished with a project, when the session must end. To help in this area, announce when there are five minutes remaining before clean-up. (Even children who aren't finished must clean up with the others.) If possible, allow the child to continue working on the project at another time, placing the necessary supplies in a little box. No one likes to get in the way of creativity. Try to work as much as is practical around time constraints.

Planning

Planning is an important part of every successful endeavor. Assess the ages, developmental levels, interests and likes of the children you are working with. Cost and availability of materials are also factors in deciding what to do. Ask yourself what your goal is: to experiment with new media, to try a new technique, to practice a learned skill, or to create a finished item. Weigh all this against time available and attention span of your young craftspeople.

What about the finished project? Kids love to have their work displayed—and not just on the refrigerator. Where might it be hung? Will it be given as a gift? If so, is a time limit necessary for completion? Will wrapping paper and card be needed? Will it be exhibited? How will it be labeled, hung, displayed? What overall theme is being expressed? Will it be sent home with a child when finished? Will it need drying time? Will it need to be wrapped to prevent breakage on the way home? Be sure to let the children know what will be done with their finished work.

Labeling Projects

Labeling finished projects is one of those seemingly little details that can take on monster proportions and actually ruin an experience. Children in the primary grades often are not able to identify their finished crafts, creating arguments over whose is whose. Some children help themselves to the finished projects they like best, regardless of whose name is on it. Try to keep finished work displayed away from the door, making sure that children retrieve their own items with adult supervision.

Displaying Work

How to best display finished projects can sometimes become a challenge. Use cardboard boxes, covered with wallpaper or paint, to create four-sided displays atop a table. Boxes can also be covered or painted, and weighted down with a brick inside, to become pedestals for display of three-dimensional work.

If children work on the same size paper most of the time, pre-cut mats work well. Display on the wall with different children's works matted each week. Nothing makes a picture quite as special as a mat or frame and a place on the wall.

Work hung on the walls can sometimes be stapled up, but if you want to avoid putting small holes in the work, and the wall, use the synthetic substance that remains adhesive and can be used over and over. Sold in the office supply section of many food and drug stores, it can be rolled back into a ball and used many times.

Recycling for Grab Art

No one likes to throw away any portion of materials that can be recycled for another project. Keep boxes for scraps of colored paper, yarn, mat board, or anything else that can be used again. Save empty shampoo bottles to store unusual shades of paint. Keep a clean covered trash can in the corner to save items for Grab Art projects.

When you have a supply of assorted bits and pieces of sequins, yarns, fabric scraps, colored tissue papers, wall paper

sample pages and whatever else, begin to fill Grab Art bags. Use brown paper lunch sacks, filling each one with assorted odds and ends. Fold over the top of each bag and staple once. When you have enough bags for everyone, you are ready for a truly creative make-it session.

Children select bags, go to their seats and open them. Using only the items found in the bag, each child creates something of his or her choice. Provide tape, glue, paste or staples, and sheets of paper or colored tagboard. Let their imaginations go wild. If some children need prompting at first, suggest a variety of things to do: puppets, bookmarks, sculptures, toys, outer space creatures, mobiles, or whatever else the materials seem to suggest.

Grab Art also helps use up the bits and pieces of supplies that are too good to throw away, but are in limited supply. Kids love Grab Art. Maybe it's because of the mystery of what is in their bag, as well as the no-holds-barred approach to creating.

Glossary

adhere: to stick or hold in place.

armature: the framework that supports a sculpture.

banner: a flag or similar piece of material with words or a special design.

brad: a round brass fastener with two bendable metal strips, used to hold paper pieces together.

brayer: a handheld roller used by a printer or artist to apply ink.

buff (v): to polish or shine.

ceramics: the art or method of making objects from clay. The clay is shaped and then baked at a high temperature.

coiling: winding around in a series of spirals or rings.

composition: the parts of an object and the way in which they are combined.

compound: a substance that is formed by combining separate substances or ingredients.

compressed: when an object is squeezed or pressed together.

consistency: the degree of how thick, thin, soft, or firm an object is.

contour: the outline of a figure, body, or mass.

crimp (v): to cause to become wavy, bent, or pinched.

cuneiform: an alphabet written in wedge-shaped characters.

cylinder: a hollow or solid object shaped like a tube or pipe.

dilute: to make weaker or more liquid, as by adding water to a substance.

dimension: the measure of length, width, or height.

disposable: an object that is thrown away, rather than reused.

dowel: a round, wooden pin used to fasten two pieces of wood together.

durable: able to withstand long wear or hard use.

emblem: an object or picture that represents something else.

emboss: to decorate with a raised design.

etch: to make a drawing or design by cutting lines with acid on a metal or glass plate.

festive: merry and joyful; suitable for a festival.

flyleaf: one of the endpapers of a book.

fossil: the remains or traces of a plant or animal embedded in rock or other material.

fragrant: having a strong, pleasing odor or smell.

free-form: having an irregular shape or design; not following a pattern.

froths (v): bubbles, foams.

geometric: made up of simple shapes formed from straight lines or curves.

glaze: a coating applied to ceramics that results in a glossy surface.

glossy: the quality of having a smooth and shiny surface.

image: a representation of a person or object; a picture or photograph of a real object.

impressionist: a painter who uses dabs or strokes of color to represent reflected light. Monet and Renoir were French impressionist artists.

incise: to cut into.

inscription: something that is written, printed, carved, or engraved in an object.

intaglio: a process in printmaking that is done from a plate in which the image is sunk below the surface.

irregular: not standard, even, or uniform in shape, size, length, or arrangement.

kiln: an oven or furnace used by potters to bake or fire clay.

latex: a substance that is used in paints, adhesives, and other objects, such as gloves.

lentil: the round, flat seed of a pod-bearing plant related to beans and peas.

marzipan: a candy made of almond paste, sugar, and egg whites that is often shaped into various forms.

matte finish: a smooth, even surface that is dull, not shiny.

medium: a means by which something is accomplished, such as the kind of materials selected in order to produce artwork.

mosaic: a design made by fitting and cementing together small pieces of hard material, such as colored glass or tile.

opaque: not capable of letting light pass through.

personalize: to make an object one's own.

pliable: easily bent or shaped without breaking; flexible.

portraiture: the making of a portrait, which is a picture of a person.

preserve: to treat an object in a certain way in order to save it.

pulp: a wet mixture of ground-up wood or rags used to make paper.

ratio: a relationship in amount, number, or size of two objects.

realistic: closely resembling real life.

silhouette: a drawing that consists of outlines that are filled in with solid color.

simulate: to imitate.

skewer: a long pin made of metal or wood that is used to fasten objects, such as pieces of meat, fruit, or vegetables, together.

slab: a broad, thick piece of a substance, such as clay or stone.

spine: the backbone of something, such as an animal or book.

squeegee: a blade of rubber or leather on a handle used for spreading, pushing, or wiping liquids on, across, or off of a surface.

still life: a picture primarily consisting of objects that cannot move.

taper: to make or become gradually thinner, such as a pencil point.

technique: a way of doing something.

template: a pattern or mold used as a guide for the shape of an object that is being made.

tendril: a slender, coiling plant part; a curl or curled end.

tesserae: small pieces of paper or other materials used in a mosaic.

Books

Adventures in Art. Susan Milord (Williamson)

Art Smart (series). Christine Smith (Gareth Stevens)

Cut-Paper Play! Sandi Henry (Williamson)

Draw, Model, and Paint (series). Isidro Sanchez (Gareth Stevens)

Easy Crafts: Things to Make at Home and School. Colin Caket (Sterling)

EcoArt! Laurie Carlson (Williamson)

Fifty Nature Projects for Kids. Cecilia Fitzsimons (Smithmark)

Fun With Paint. Moira Butterfield (Random House)

Fun With Paper Bags and Cardboard Tubes. Virginia Walter (Sterling)

Hand-Print Animal Art. Carolyn Carreiro (Williamson)

Kids' Computer Creations: Using Your Computer for Art & Craft Fun. Carol Sabbeth (Williamson)

Kids' Crazy Concoctions: 50 Mysterious Mixtures for Art & Craft Fun. Jill Frankel Hauser (Williamson)

The Kids' Multicultural Art Book. Williamson Kids Can!® (series). Alexandra M. Terzian (Gareth Stevens)

The Little Hands Art Book. Judy Press (Williamson)

Making Cool Crafts & Awesome Art! Roberta Gould (Williamson)

Prints. Judy Ann Sadler (Kids Can Press)

Sixty Art Projects for Children. Jeannette M. Baumgardner (Clarkson Potter)

Snips & Snails & Walnut Whales: Nature Crafts for Children. Phyllis Fiarotta (Workman)

Worldwide Crafts (series). (Gareth Stevens)

Young Naturalist Field Guides (series). (Gareth Stevens)

Young Scientist Concepts and Projects (series). (Gareth Stevens)

Videos

Crafts and Activities for Kids. (GoodTimes Home Video Corporation)

Fun With Heritage Crafts. (Creative Pastimes in Video)

Fun With Paints. (Creative Pastimes in Video)

Kids' Do-It-Yourself Projects. (GoodTimes Home Video Corporation)

Kids 'n' Craft Series: Fun With Clay, Make a Puppet, Paper Play, Make a Print. (Morris Video)

Let's Create Fun Jewelry for Boys and Girls. (Crystal Productions)

Look What I Made: Paper Playthings and Gifts, My First Activity Video. (Sony)

My Fun Pack: Fun With Clay. (Morris Video)

Neat Stuff to Make for Kids. (GoodTimes Home Video Corporation)

Origami for Kids. (Media Methods)

Paper Play. (Morris Video)

Places to Visit

American Folk Art Museum
Two Lincoln Square
Columbus Avenue
New York, NY 10023

Art Institute of Chicago
111 South Michigan Avenue
Chicago, IL 60603-6110

**Canadian Museum of
    Civilization**
100 Laurier Street
P. O. Box 3100, Station B
Hull, Quebec
J8X 4H2

**Denver Museum of
    Natural History**
2001 Colorado Boulevard
Denver, CO 80205

The Franklin Institute
20th Street and the Franklin Parkway
Philadelphia, PA 19103-1194

High Museum of Art
1280 Peachtree Street, N.E.
Atlanta, GA 30309

**Los Angeles County
    Museum of Art**
5905 Wilshire Boulevard
Los Angeles, CA 90036

Metropolitan Museum of Art
1000 Fifth Avenue
New York, NY 10028

Milwaukee Public Museum
800 West Wells Street
Milwaukee, WI 53201

**National Jewish Children's
    Art Museum**
National Jewish Medical and
    Research Center
1400 Jackson Street
Denver, CO 80206

Royal British Columbia Museum
675 Belleville Street
Victoria, British Columbia
V8V 1X4

The Smithsonian Institution
1000 Jefferson Drive, S.W.
Washington, D.C. 20560

Web Sites

www.burrows.com/found.html

frontpage.lightspeed.net/
    oracle/artcraft.htm

www2.best.com/~jantypas/

www.hukilau.com/art/

www.he.net/~sparker/cranes.html

www.exploratorium.edu/

Some web sites stay current longer than others. For further web sites, use your search engines to locate the following topics: *art, balloons, candles, crafts, papier mâché, printmaking,* and *salt dough.*

Index

A

alphabets 47
ammonia 108
animal crackers 135
apples
    balloon 107
    people 118-119
    tree print 56
Assyrians 47
autumn projects
    115-130

B

bags, paper
    25, 28, 94, 126
balloons
    in papier mâché 69-72
    people 18
    sculpture 106-107
balls, Christmas 138
banners, wall 141
barrettes, hair 40
beads
    clay 40
    paper 29
beans, lima 124
bells, winter 138
binding, book 13
bird in a cage 88

bluing 108
bowls, papier-mâché
    68
bracelets 30
brayers 53, 57-59
bread 43
bubble-wrap 66
bubbles 113
buttons 41

C

cactus, salt dough 50
calligraphy 16
candles
    dipped 130
    sand 102
candy houses 142-143
cards, pop-up 12
carolers 140
cartons
    egg 6, 57, 127
    milk 128, 142
chalk 33
charcoal 108
Christmas crafts
    134-138, 140-144
      candles 144
      decorations 144
      ornaments 138
Cinco de Mayo 93
clay
    barrettes, hair 40
    beads 40
    bread 43

buttons 41
dishes, slab 34, 35
    homemade 42
    pinch pots 34
    pottery, coiled 36
    salt dough 43-52
    sawdust 42
    tablet 47
clipboards 96
clips, paper 65
clothespins 96
cloves 135
collages, Indian corn
    117
concrete operations stages
    149
cookie cutters 39, 44
counts, winter 25
cradles, oatmeal box
    122
crayons
    cookies 89
    scratchboard 89
crystal gardens 108
cut-paper art
    cut-paper mosaic 23
    weave pictures 23

D

detergent, dish
    113, 132
dinosaurs 70-73
    bone 73
    egg 72

    papier-mâché 70-71
dogs
    bank 111
    invisible 109
dolls, corn husk 120
dough, salt 43-47

E

eggs
    dinosaur 72
    Easter 84
    robin 81
eggshell mosaic
    83
embossing 16
envelopes 11

F

fabric 13, 19, 78, 121
feathers 11
felt 141
finger paints 54, 60-61
fish prints 55
flyleaf 13
foam rubber 109
foil, aluminum
    24, 30, 50, 51
      sculpture 75
food printing 55
fossils 37
frames, picture 139
frosting 142-143